Cruise Sunlit Sea-trails the Union Way

UNION STEAMSHIPS

THE GOOD COMPANY

THE GOOD COMPANY

An Affectionate History of the Union Steamships

Tom Henry

❖

Harbour Publishing

Harbour Publishing
PO Box 219,
Madeira Park, BC Canada V0N 2H0

Published with the assistance of the Canada Council and the Government of British Columbia, Tourism and Ministry Responsible for Culture, Cultural Services Branch.

Cover painting by Michael Dean
Back cover painting and chapter illustrations by Graham Wragg
Cover design, page design and composition by Roger Handling
Printed and bound in Canada

Canadian Cataloguing in Publication Data

Henry, Tom, 1961-
The good company

ISBN 1-55017-111-9

1. Union Steamship Company of British Columbia– History.
2. Steamboats– British Columbia – Pacific Coast – History. I.
Title.
HE945.U5H46 1994   387.2'044'060711   C94-910737-9

Photo Credits

Pages 2–3, 23, 66–67: Stuart Thomson, courtesy of City of Vancouver Archives (CVA); 14 (middle and bottom), 16, 17 (top right), 20–21, 23, 36 (middle), 38–39, 43 (bottom), 47, 66 (top), 70–71, 74–75, 85, 94 (top & middle left), 101 (top), 103 (bottom), 106 (top l.), 112 (top), 116 (top), 134: City of Vancouver Archives; 15, 17 (bottom), 38–39, 40, 42 (top), 63, 77, 78, 118 (top), 139 (bottom): James Crookall (CVA); 5, 24 (bottom), 26, 29 (bottom), 30, 33, 36 (top right), 46, 49 (middle & bottom), 54, 55, 56, 61, 73 (top l. & r.), 76 (bottom), 79, 88, 89 (bottom), 90, 96 (top), 107 (top), 109, 112 (bottom), 116 (bottom), 117, 118, 126, 127, 132 (bottom), 136, 140, 141: courtesy of Art Twigg (AT); 14 (top), 17 (top left), 18, 19, 22 (top), 25, 28 (top), 32 (top & bottom left), 36 (top left & bottom), 37, 39, 43 (top l. & r.), 48 (top), 49 (top), 50 (top), 52, 57, 58–59, 60, 62, 64, 67, 68–69; 72 (top), 73 (bottom), 76 (top), 80, 82 (bottom), 84, 86–87, 92, 94–95, 95, 96 (lower & middle), 97, 98, 100, 101 (bottom), 102, 103 (top), 104–105, 106 (top r.), 108, 110 (bottom), 110–111, 111 (bottom), 114, 119, 120–121, 122, 123, 125, 128, 129 (bottom), 137, 138, 139 (top r. & l.): Vancouver Maritime Museum (VMM); 22 (bottom), 24 (top), 48 (lower): Elphinstone Museum; 28–29 (bottom): Walter E. Frost (CVA); 31: Link and Pin Museum; 32 (bottom right): P.J. Hall (AT); 34–35, 42 (bottom): Leonard Frank (AT); 44–45: David Bee (AT); 50–51: Campbell River Museum & Archives; 71: BC Archives & Records Service; 72 (bottom): courtesy of Jim Spilsbury; 82 (top): A. C. Phillips (AT); 82–83, 89 (top), 93, 129 (top), 131 (bottom): Clinton H. Betz (AT); 107 (middle l.): Leonard Frank (CVA); 107 (middle r.): A.E. Hill (CVA); 110 (top): W.J. Moore (CVA); 113, 130, 131 (top), 132 (top): Jack Lindsay (CVA); 124: Imperial War Museum.

CONTENTS

On her summertime excursions along the south coast, the *Lady Alexandra* was often loaded to the gunwales with tourists.

Union Steamships Remembered

O ne day in the late 1980s maritime artist Michael Dean was showing his paintings and sketches at a mall in Campbell River. Dean, whose watercolour graces the cover of this book, was chatting with passers-by when he noticed something unusual. Instead of milling around his work, as they usually do, people were clustered around one sketch. The sketch was of the *Lady Rose*, a former Union Steamship Co. of BC vessel. Dean had just completed it. Everyone was studying the work intensely, like they would if searching for themselves or friends in an old class photo. Dean strolled over and found the picture had uncorked the past. "They kept asking if I had done pictures of the *Catala*, or the *Chelohsin*, or other Union ships," he recalled. "They had very fond memories of travelling the coast in Union boats, and they wanted to talk about it."

It is a measure of the Union company's role in coastal history that it elicits such affection and attention more than three decades after the fleet was sold (in January, 1959). For seventy years the company was such an integral part of the coast that its black hulls, its imported Scottish pound cake and its signature whistle—one long, two short, one long—became viscerally imbedded in those who rode and worked aboard the ships. Union steamers carried pregnant mothers from upcoast communities to Vancouver hospitals and lugged all the hardware (bootleg and otherwise) for pioneer living from Vancouver to upcoast communities. And they did so with a distinctive style. What other company would have summoned caulk-booted loggers to dinner with a multi-toned dinner gong, or featured skippers as conversant in the language of the new country (Chinook) as they were in the language of the old country (Gaelic)?

Only in the last decade has the Union's effect on the larger character of the coast become clear. Its routes—radiating out from Vancouver like spokes in a wheel—had the effect of making even the smallest stump and mud settlement an adjunct of the province's largest metropolitan centre. Thus Woodwards wedding cake was as common in Kingcome Inlet as it was in Kitsilano, and loggers were as familiar with city mores as they were with bunkhouse manners. A company that became an institution: It is no exaggeration to say that

With its rail and sea connections, Vancouver harbour was the vital link between the coastal pioneers and the outside world.

the Union company did for the coast what the CPR did for the country.

This book owes a great deal to two former Union men, Gerald Rushton and Art Twigg. Rushton, an upper middle class Englishman with a background in the classics, was a manager with the company for four decades. After the firm sold its fleet he wrote a history, the rigorously detailed 'Whistle Up The Inlet'. It is primarily a business history, based on Rushton's inside access to corporate goings-on. Today, with company records widely dispersed or simply vanished, it is impossible to conceive of a Union book that wouldn't be indebted at some level to Rushton's work. I acknowledge that debt.

For all his knowledge of the corporate goings on, though, Rushton was not intimately versed in life aboard Union ships. Like most Union company executives, he fancied the company as a model of British efficiency, which it was decidedly not. In the mornings, Gerald Rushton used to march from his office down to the Union dock to query pursers on the passenger counts. Union ships usually departed for upcoast destinations in the mornings and pursers (or assistant pursers) were supposed to stand beside each gangplank, take tickets, and keep tally of the passenger counts. Rushton would stride up with a military demeanor and say "Good morning! What's the count today?" The purser would bark back the number, ideally suffixed with a crisp "Sir!" "Very good!" Rushton would say, then stride off to the next gangplank.

That was the theory, anyway. In reality, pursers were often late to arrive, or

The *Coquitlam*, going astern as it leaves the Union dock, passes the *Cardena* on its way to northern ports.

if they did happen in early they were too busy yakking with officers around the mess table to tend to that particular duty. So they devised a system where several pursers stood in for the ones who weren't there. As soon as one purser was finished with Rushton he'd scoot behind the manager's back, down the dock, and take a spot in front of the next gangplank. And so it went, two or three pursers circling round and round the oblivious Rushton, relay-like, until he was done his count (which, of course, was based on best guesses of the pursers). It was efficiency, just not the kind company executives had in mind. Typical Union.

That anecdote comes from the other Union employee, Art Twigg. Twigg had an insider's position in the company too, though his was from the vantage of the ships. For the best part of the 1940s Twigg worked as a freight clerk, assistant purser and purser aboard Union vessels. He worked aboard every ship in the fleet, and alongside most of the company's legendary characters. Through his own notes, made on board, and hundreds of hours of interviews he conducted with former Union employees years later, Twigg has created an archive of informal, offbeat and unofficial company history. It's good stuff, put together by a good man. To him this book is especially indebted.

Other individuals and organizations were also instrumental in the writing of this book. Leonard McCann, Curator Emeritus of the Vancouver Maritime Museum, demonstrated that his knowledge of matters relating to ships is astounding. He unearthed archival material and photos, and made many valuable suggestions. The staff of the

Vancouver City Archives, the Vancouver Maritime Museum and the BC Archives and Records Services were of great assistance and always enthusiastic. (BCARS charitably gave permission to quote from its booklet of the Union Steamship Co., 'Navigating the Coast'.) Stephanie Crosbie was an exceptional researcher, even under pressure of deadline. Bruce and Jan Davidson provided a quiet place to work, and a woodstove to keep it warm on chill mornings. And finally, Lorna Jackson's editing and thoughtful suggestions improved the text immeasurably.

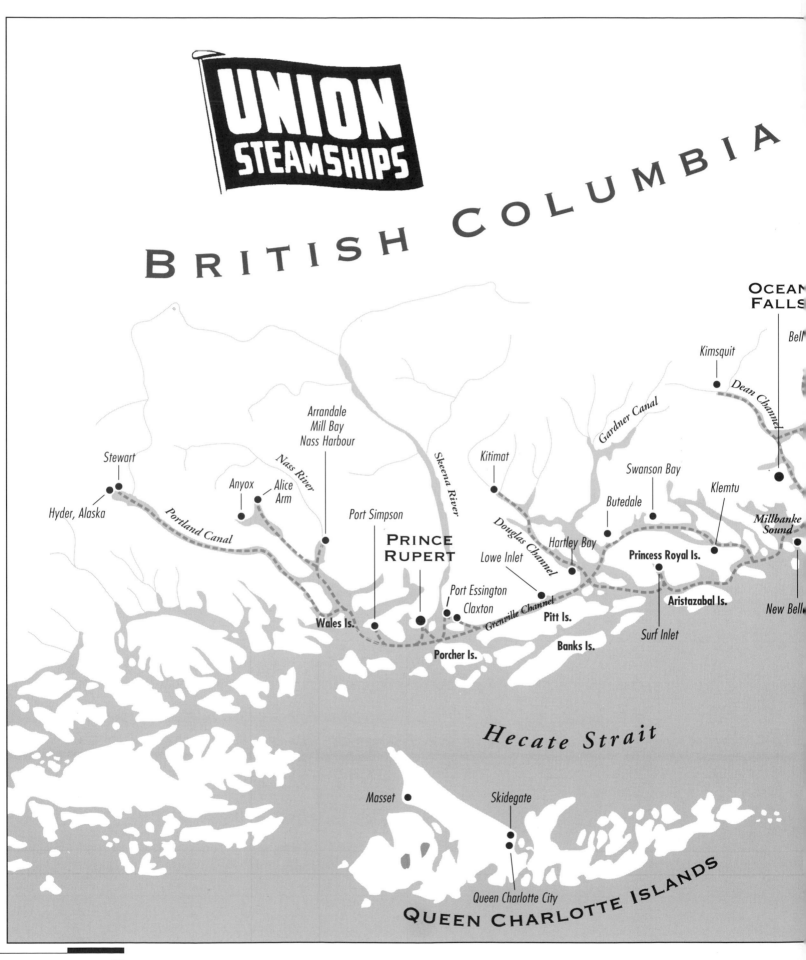

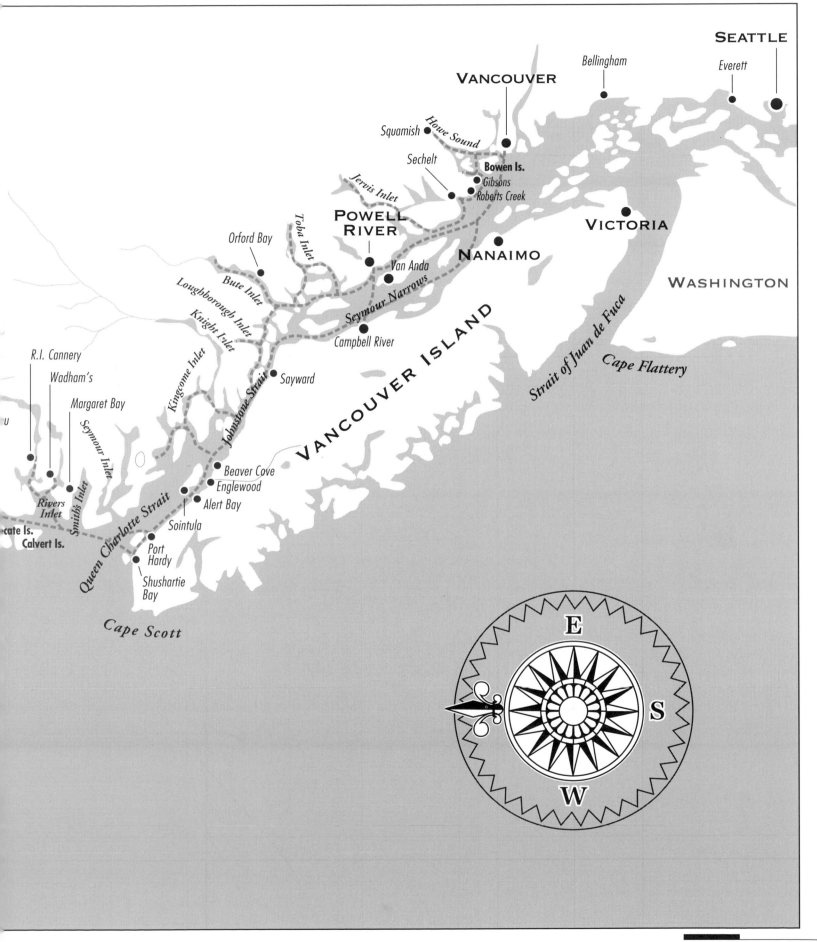

SEATTLE

Bellingham

Everett

VANCOUVER

Squamish

Howe Sound

Sechelt

Bowen Is.

Gibsons

Roberts Creek

Jervis Inlet

POWELL
RIVER

VICTORIA

Orford Bay

Toba Inlet

Van Anda

NANAIMO

WASHINGTON

Bute Inlet

Seymour Narrows

Loughborough Inlet

Knight Inlet

Campbell River

VANCOUVER ISLAND

Strait of Juan de Fuca

Cape Flattery

R.I. Cannery

Sayward

Wadham's

Johnstone Strait

Kingcome Inlet

Margaret Bay

u

Seymour Inlet

Beaver Cove

Englewood

Alert Bay

Rivers
Inlet

Smiths Inlet

Sointula

cate Is.

Calvert Is.

Queen Charlotte Strait

Port
Hardy

Shushartie
Bay

Cape Scott

E

S

W

Chapter One

1889-1900:
Ships and Men

"Do you mean to say," the Captain was asked, "that you know where every reef, rock and sandbar is in these waters?"
"No," he replied, "but I know where they ain't."
Anonymous

Histion depends on who does the telling. For author Gerald Rushton, the seminal event in the history of the Union Steamship Company of British Columbia was the arrival in Vancouver, in 1888, of John Darling. Darling was a director and retired general superintendent of the prosperous Union Steamship Co. of New Zealand and, according to Rushton, needed little more than a glance at Burrard Inlet—where a band of ramshackle little steamers struggled to meet the demands of a booming lumber industry—to imagine the opportunities for a local shipping firm. He assembled a group of local businessmen to finance the project and on July 1, 1889, the Union Steamship Co. of BC was formed, launching not only a major shipping company in the province but also, according to Rushton, a coastal institution.

Gerald Rushton worked as a manager in the Union company's clapboard office at the foot of Carrall Street, in Vancouver. Those men who worked and ate and slept aboard Union ships marked the company's genesis from a different date: May 2, 1892. Late in the morning of that day, the Union's SS *Comox* finished loading an eclectic cargo that included barrels of beer, groceries, feed, hay, oil, mail, sides of beef and crates and crates of squealing pigs and squawking chickens. With a signal from Capt. Charles Moody, an affable, yarn-spinning Newfoundlander, the ship's Manila lines were cast off and the vessel eased its way out of the First Narrows, past Point Atkinson, and swung north into the Strait of Georgia.

The *Comox* was bound for Port Neville, on Johnstone Strait. A hand-hewn, stump-and-mud settlement, Port Neville was the most distant in a series of some twenty

**Opposite:
An excursion party on the Union Steamship *Cutch* while cruising in Howe Sound, 1892. The Master of the vessel at the time was Captain Johnson (top centre).**

Union founder John Darling arrived in Vancouver following a cross-Canada train trip with CPR president and legendary railwayman (later Sir) William Van Horne.

Below: A crowded Union dock on Dominion Day, 1890. The Union tug *Skidegate* is about to tow a scow load of passengers to Brockton Point for a day of sports. Two more barges (foreground, right) will leave in the next 30 minutes. Round trip cost 25 cents. Large vessel in the background is probably the recently acquired *Cutch*.
Bottom: Vessels from around the world sailed to Vancouver Harbour to take on lumber from the Hastings and Moodyville sawmills.

logging "centres" and camps that had sprung up along the coast north of the Fraser River. These operations included two camps on Howe Sound, McPherson's and Gillis's; Dineen's on Jervis Inlet; William McKay at Grief Point; Ireland and Leatherdale at Lewis Channel; King & Casey near Campbell River; and Angus McCallum's camp at Sayward. And between these big establishments, scores of handloggers were scouring the bays and bluffs for easily accessible fir and cedar. Altogether, there were perhaps a thousand loggers at work, with more coming all the time.

Until the *Comox* began regular service, starting with that May 2 run, these loggers had to provide their own transportation, or rely on the whims of Victoria- and New Westminster-based steamer companies—who tended to look to Puget Sound and the Fraser River for business—to send a vessel freelancing into the area. It was a lousy situation for employers and employees, who often found themselves stuck together against their wishes in a wet, no-name inlet, praying for a steamer to chance in and break the purgatory of a bad relationship. Little wonder the *Comox* was booked solid from the beginning.

Fact is, the Union company would never have survived infancy, let alone grown to be an "institution," had the *Comox* and Captain Moody not made that May 2 trip. The Union company was not in good shape in its first years; in their attempts to capitalize on Vancouver's booming economy the Union's directors sent it off on several Quixote-like sprees that saw it get into all sorts of trouble.

The *Comox* at Irvine's Landing, in Pender Harbour. Success of such runs helped extract the Union company from the financial crisis of the early 1890s.

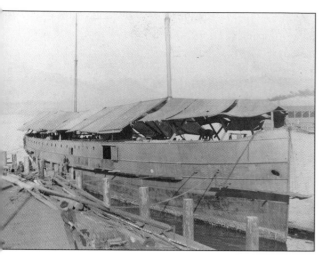

One of these unsuccessful ventures was a regular service from Vancouver to Nanaimo. For this the company had acquired the SS *Cutch*, a rakish, two-funnel steamer, built in 1884 as a yacht for the Maharaja of Cutch, an Indian prince. The Rajah died soon after the ship was built, and it bounced, via a group of Indian merchants and the German government, into the hands of a Bombay dealer named Hajeebhoy Lalljee. He sold it to the Union company's first manager, the unfortunate Capt. William Webster, who sailed immediately for Vancouver.

The *Cutch* arrived on June 2, 1890. Within a month it was put into competition on the Vancouver–Nanaimo run against the Dunsmuir family's steamer *Robert Dunsmuir*. Known as the "Dirty Bob," the *Robert Dunsmuir* had enjoyed virtually competition-free business carrying passengers and cargo

In order to compete with other shipping firms for the lucrative Klondike traffic, the *Cutch* was refitted (and one funnel removed) at BC Iron Works in May, 1898.

between the two growing ports. A highly publicized rivalry developed quickly between the two ships, with skippers and crew engaged in all-out efforts to best the other vessel's performance. In the first year, the *Cutch* had the advantage, but then the Dirty Bob was replaced with a more spacious ship, the SS *City of Nanaimo*. After the new vessel bested the *Cutch* on two consecutive trips, the crew of the *Cutch* announced in the *Vancouver Daily News-Advertiser* they were going to beach the ship, scrape its hull, and return to the run to "knock the spots" off the competition.

Above: Nanaimo's waterfront also boomed in the 1890s. Here the *Cutch* eases into Johnston's Wharf, near the present CPR dock.

Right: When not on the Vancouver–Nanaimo run, the *Cutch* was in great demand for excursions. The notice for one outing to Victoria read: "No person will be allowed on board without a ticket. The *Cutch* leaves at 6 a.m. sharp and no one will be waited for!"

The battle between the two ships came to a roaring end when, on November 12, 1892, while attempting to catch up to the *City of Nanaimo*, the *Cutch* did a hit-and-run in Nanaimo harbour on another Dunsmuir vessel, the SS *Joan*. Tried in the Exchequer Court, the Union company had to ante up for repairs to the *Joan*, plus suffer a public scolding from the judge, Chief Justice Sir Matthew Baillie Begbie.

(The *Cutch*'s trying relationship with the Union company lasted for ten years. During the height of the Klondike gold rush, when the company was trying to cash in on thousands of men who wanted to get north, the *Cutch* smacked into Horseshoe Reef, twenty-five miles south of Juneau, Alaska. Although the *Cutch* was to be salvaged, the Union company decided to rid itself of the aging ship and settled for £6,000 insurance.)

Running at a maximum speed of 14 knots, the *Cutch* made the 1100-mile trip from Vancouver to Skagway, Alaska (left and above) in 88 hours.

Left: According to the *Cutch*'s captain the ship "experienced dirty weather, wet and thick" before running aground on Horseshoe Reef. The ship was salvaged and sold to Colombia, where it became the government gunboat *Bogota*.

During its first years, the Union company also became embroiled in an international fiasco that was to take over three decades to resolve. This involved the SS *Coquitlam*, one of three ships along with the *Comox* and the *Capilano*, the company had ordered soon after it was formed. Manufactured in Scotland, the vessels were shipped to BC in pieces and reassembled on makeshift ways at Vancouver's Coal Harbour.

The last and largest of the three pre-fab vessels the Union company assembled in Vancouver's Coal Harbour, the *Coquitlam* cruised at an economical 30 miles per ton of coal.

The *Coquitlam* was launched in April 1892. One month later it was chartered by BC Sealers to supply their schooners working off Alaska. At the time, there was tremendous tension between Canada and the US over sealing rights, and this resulted in the impounding of the *Coquitlam* on June 22. Although the action was later declared wrongful, the case dragged through the muck of international diplomacy for twenty-nine years before the Union saw any money.

Most disastrous, however, was the company's venture into the area of deep-sea shipping. In 1891, company manager Capt. William Webster entered into a contract with the CPR to ferry passengers and cargo from Vancouver to Portland, where the CPR's Empress ocean liners regularly called. For this the company chartered—at great expense—two vessels, the SS *Tai Chow* and the SS *Grandholm*. From the beginning the service was a flop. Captain Webster hadn't counted on competition from the Upton Line, which was taking much of the CPR's cross-Pacific business. The ships regularly carried more crew than passengers, and more coal than cargo. As the Union drifted further into debt, Webster claimed the CPR had guaranteed against loss. The CPR would hear none of it. By the time the company cleared itself of the deal, it owed the Bank of BC forty thousand dollars. That was money the Union didn't have.

Facing bankruptcy, the company's directors issued, in 1893, what has to be one of the most pathetic annual reports in Canadian commercial history. They first suggested the losses were a result of a smallpox epidemic and general "tightness of money" in the economy. Then they admitted the source of the crisis, but glossed it over with the brave declaration that they had "resolved to send Capt. Webster, the Manager of the Company, to

England, as he was fully conversant with the reasons of the loss, having made the contract with the CPR, and having carried it out as Manager, to explain the whole position to the English shareholders...." Finally (and this is in the space of three pages), the directors came clean. They needed current shareholders to put up the forty thousand or "your Directors can't hold out much hope for the future."

Against this backdrop of confusion and botched ventures, the *Comox*'s up-coast run emerged as one of the few money-making enterprises. At first, its loosely structured weekly route included Gibson's Landing, Sechelt, Welcome Pass, Van Anda, Comox, Lund, Manson's Landing, Read Island, Stuart Island and stops up-coast as far north as Port Neville. Within two years there was so much demand the *Comox* was put on a twice-weekly schedule, leaving Vancouver on Mondays and Thursdays. Not only was the company making money, but for the *Comox*'s service the Dominion government granted the company an annual subsidy of sixty thousand dollars.

When not servicing upcoast logging operations, the *Comox* took holidaying parties to Bowen Island.

Remember that history depends on who does the telling, and an account of a round trip, written in 1894 by a "W.F.G." and published by the company, suggests not only how quickly the *Comox* became an essential part of coastal life; the little essay also serves as a romantic steamship portrait—endorsed by the Union Steamship Co.:

> *"I was assured that the boat, if not of the tonnage of a man-of-war, was roomy enough for taking exercise, that the meals, though plain, would be plentiful and well served, the berths clean, and our fellow travellers, if destitute of collars and cuff, perfectly civil...."*

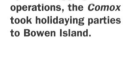

Leaving Vancouver, July 1898.

The first steel ship built in BC, the *Comox* added a brisk, modern air to Vancouver's waterfront. Here it is off Brockton Point, inbound for the Union dock.

With two upcoast runs a week, the *Comox* was often in and out of the Union dock in hours.

"[W]e took passage at the Union Steamship Co's wharf at 11 on a radiant summer morning, and the fresh breeze of Burrard Inlet soon inspired a feeling of buoyancy and vigour, especially to one who had but recently spent several days on the railway cars....

"Our first stopping place is Gibson's Landing, at the west entrance of Howe Sound. On the north is descried Bowen Island, teeming with deer, and beyond, Anvil Island, named after its shape. Mr. Gibson at his landing,—the tide being low,—'yanks' ashore the cow and calf we have brought, by the simple method of persuading them sternly into the water and inducing them to swim to land. Outside lie Paisley and Ragged Islands, sometime the camps of whalers who harpooned these waters profitably. The plateau of Popham Island confronts us, showing where the adventurers kept watch for their shoals of victims...."

"W.F.G." provides more than a simple advertisement for a "Weekly Cruise" through British Columbia waters. He writes stylishly of the up-coast cultures and lifestyles that, without the service of steamboats, would remain disconnected and ultimately forgotten in the history of BC. His trip continues:

"...past occasional shanties and clearances that skirt the shores of Georgia's Gulf, past Trail Bay, until our good ship signals on Sechelt Village, an Indian settlement where we have to put ashore the Roman Catholic Bishop. Canoes contending for the honor are soon alongside and the dignitary is landed to the strains of music furnished by the native band, whose members are shining like the stars, in gold lace on a firmament of blue cloth....As we sail through Welcome pass...the sun is setting in wealth of color over the north end of Texada Island...All about these waters, it should be said, the gentle angler can find captives to his spear or spoon-bait. Salmon teem round the shores, and big trout are sporting in the inland streams."

Writer Joseph Conrad, an able and experienced seaman who longed for the day of the sailing ship to carry on forever, complained long and hard about the horrific noise and clattering disruption aboard steamships. But on BC's waters, "W.F.G." chronicles a romantic voyage even the nostalgic Conrad could take to: "...But night has fallen and the moon is over the island-studded reaches of the strait, 'the shining sensitive silver of the sea' is round about, and as the boat pursues her almost noiseless course through the silent channels we are lured to sleep. Sleep should not, however, hold us long....

Early Union stops included the mission at Sechelt.

"[W]e relinquish our comfortable berths, braving the contempt of the deck hands for our needlessly early hours, as we enter Evans Bay on Head Island, and put ashore to the lonely ranchman his welcome mail. The steamboat shortly enters the Hole-in-the-wall....The tide runs fast and the ship needs careful steering, but the captain is on deck, and we are soon amongst the logging camps again delivering huge sides of beef and bales of hay, and letters from friends to the lonely camps of loggers who look us a welcome as they shoot out from shore in their motley crafts, and return with their spoil....

"The return voyage from Port Neville begins at mid-day....And so leaving behind in the boat's track a succession of small settlements and more lumber camps, where teams comprising 16 or more huge patient oxen haul down the forest giants, whilst big hirsute men with spiked boots and long poles dance over the floating logs as they arrange them into booms, our route is varied somewhat from our up-going trip."

Half a century after the original *Comox* made its first upcoast run, the *Comox II* was carrying full loads of passengers to Whytecliff Park.

As the first ship on the coast to maintain a regular route into the small logging camps and out-of-the-way settlements on the coast, the *Comox* served as a navigation school for future Union officers. The area it served—the craggy, island-littered mass of bays and channels between Vancouver Island and the mainland—is one of the most difficult areas on the coast to navigate. Tides sweep through at speeds of up to 12 knots, creating a twisting jumble of eddies and back eddies capable of jarring the largest liners. Winds roar down from

Fog didn't hinder the best Union navigators, who relied on a combination of sound, timing and sixth sense to guide their ships up shrouded inlets and passageways. The only time the whistle failed was in snow, which deadened echoes.

the long inlets, whipping up a treacherous chop, or in cold weather, creating dangerous icing conditions that have sunk more than one ship.

Capt. Charles Moody, it was said, was one of those Newfoundland shipmasters to whom navigation comes as a birthday gift. During the 1890s, Moody and other Union navigators like him perfected two navigational techniques that were to be used for the next fifty years. The first was the maintenance of exact logbooks. As a Union ship made its way through the morass of islands, regular notation of time, tide and bearing was made in a logbook. In winding inlets it wasn't unusual for navigators to record ten navigation changes in ten minutes. Thus, when the ship had to run the same route in the dark, or when visibility was poor, navigators could follow the course set out by the previous passage. As long as the speed of the ship was constant, the same course and time could be used over and over. The terse notations were sometimes accompanied by sketches of mountaintops, or other prominent geography that might help a navigator find his way.

Capt. James Findlay.

Backing up this rudimentary navigational system was the ship's whistle. When Union vessels ran in the fog, the navigator regularly sounded the whistle then counted the seconds until he heard the echo. Union skippers usually figured on sound travelling a mile in five and a half seconds. If the echo took eleven seconds then they knew they were a mile off: five and a half seconds to go ashore and five and a half seconds to come back. Many rounded this out to twelve seconds. If they got the whistle back in three seconds, they knew they were a quarter mile off; six seconds, half a mile off, and so on.

Over time, Union navigators became remarkably adept at using the whistle to pinpoint their position anywhere on the coast. They could "read" the surrounding terrain—bluffs, wooded mountains, valleys— by the varying resonances of the echo. And the very best navigators, such as Captain Moody, claimed they could get echoes from fish boats, rocks, even deadheads.

To sailors used to the expanses of the open ocean, this system of navigation seemed ludicrous. One early Union navigator recalled his shock at discovering the captain leaning over the rail of his vessel, scanning the water with a light. When asked what he was doing, the captain answered he was looking for something he called the "white rock." Calmly, he explained that's how he would know when to change course. Another early navigator, James Findlay, joined the company after years on sailing vessels. He had a square-rig certificate which, theoretically, was a licence to command any ship anywhere in the world. Findlay took a quick look at what "W.F.G." might regard as the "interminable labyrinth of watery lanes" the Union vessels were sailing through and decided to take a position as third mate while he learned the tricks of navigating the coast. When his ship was in an up-coast harbour he'd take a dinghy and lead line and take his own soundings.

In addition to the whistle and logbook, Union navigators developed what can only be described as a sixth sense for where they were. George Gaisford was one such navigator. Trained aboard the *Comox*, he was able to locate the ship's position anywhere on the coast by the smell of the air. Another early captain was able to tell, to within one degree, the direction the ship was pointing even while dozing in his bunk.

Before 1920 there were few official aids to navigation. Instead, ships relied on residents. A minister at Van Anda, for example, used to put a lamp outside his house to help ships locate the harbour. In Whaletown, Mrs. Thompson regularly put a light on certain rocks to help ships navigate the difficult passage from Whaletown to Manson's Landing.

Over the years the *Comox* remained remarkably accident free. This streak ended on April 22, 1901, when it piled up on the rocks in the Gut in Frederick Arm. It was late evening and the *Comox* was southbound. The first mate, James Bartlett, spotted what appeared to be a light at the end of a dock. A light usually indicated the steamer was to come and pick someone up. In this instance, however, it turned out the light wasn't at the end of the dock. It was ashore, in the postmaster's residence; the postmaster had gone to sleep with his light on. The steamer missed the dock, got caught in a current and lost its propeller on a rock. Then it was driven hard aground.

Two weeks later, the *Comox* was refloated and Captain Moody sailed back to Vancouver under steam. The *Comox* was given a thorough checkover and the following night the ship steamed out of First Narrows with a capacity load of passengers and cargo.

The Union's clapboard wharf office, about 1906. The company's managing director, Gordon T. Legg, is in the middle; company secretary (and later renowned photographer) James Crookall is on the far right.

Chapter Two

1901-1908:
Cassiar and Camosun

Vancouver,
CPR,
Tommy Roberts,
Cassiar.
Loggers' poem

Opposite:
One of the Union's most well-known and able navigators, the unflappable Capt. Bob Wilson. When asked by a distraught crewman if their vessel was going to make a certain tide, Wilson told him calmly not to fret. "There's lots more tides in the book," he said.

By 1900, business on the Union Steamship Company's logging camp runs had grown to such proportions that the little *Comox*, already making two trips northward a week, was unable to keep up with demand. Not only were there the existing legions of handloggers and camps to supply, but more were pouring in by the week. This influx was a result of two factors. Ontario and Quebec, facing a depletion of Crown timber reserves, had just implemented legislation prohibiting the export of raw logs to the US, which had almost exhausted its own eastern forests. At the same time the American government, under President Theodore Roosevelt, was enacting conservation legislation aimed at protecting national forests. The combined effect of the two moves was to squeeze investment north and westward. In a single two-year period at the turn of the century, BC granted over fifteen thousand timber leases.

In response to this boom, in January 1901 the company bought the wooden hull of the ex-steamer *J.R. McDonald*. The *J.R. McDonald* had been launched at Lake's Yard, Ballard, Washington on March 13, 1890, and subsequently worked carrying limestone in the San Juan Islands. On February 23, 1893, while en route from Vancouver to Seattle, it was gutted by fire and beached. Engines and boilers were removed and the hull was used to barge lumber from Burrard Inlet to Skagway during the gold rush.

During the summer of 1901, the *J.R. McDonald* was converted back into a steamer. New engines—Bow McLachlan direct-acting, inverted surface condensing steam engines—were installed, as were bunkers for 44 tons of coal. At a coal consumption rate of

The *J.R. McDonald* before the fire of 1893.

17.5 miles per ton, this gave the vessel a range of almost four hundred miles. Cabins and electricity were also added, along with something described as a "loggers' saloon." This was a warehouse of open berths, plus smoking room and bar, for woodsmen looking for economical fare to or from the camps. A small jail was also installed. Launched on Saturday, September 28, 1901, this ship was rechristened the *Cassiar*.

The *Cassiar*, or the "loggers' palace," as it came to be called, is probably the single most famous of all Union Steamship vessels. Blunt-nosed and chunky, it looked like a cantankerous old logger who had taken one too many right hooks. And sometimes it behaved like one. When the weather got too rough, the pilothouse shuddered as if battling the DTs. Its engines were no less miserable, and had a habit of sticking at inopportune times. Like when the ship was docking. The *Cassiar* would steam past a group of dumbfounded onlookers, right onto the beach, then the ship's crew would herd the passengers to the stern, where their combined weight would lift the bow, and the *Cassiar* would slide back into the water.

A more endearing feature was its wooden hull. Credited with "finding" many of the hidden reefs and rocks along the coast, it withstood bumps and bangs better than any steel hull. For example, in January 1910, while coming out of Surge Narrows, off the northeastern shore of Quadra Island, the *Cassiar* was caught by the tide and pinned against a rock with such force it couldn't move for several hours. The impact might well have buckled metal plate, but the *Cassiar*'s timbers simply flexed like cartilage until the current ebbed, and the ship continued on its way to Vancouver. Damage was nothing more than a little lost paint.

But the *Cassiar*'s real reputation was earned transporting loggers. Over the years it carried just about every coastal logger of consequence and many who weren't: Panicky Bell, Roughhouse Pete, Dog-Face Joe, Ten Spot, Bullshit Bill, Black Angus Macdonald, Spooky Charlie Lundman, Pegleg Whitey Hoolan. These men migrated with the regularity of Canada geese between the filthy, wet slopes of up-coast inlets and the warm, smoky saloons of the Tommy Roberts Grand Hotel, or the Exeter or any of the other watering holes along Carrall and Cordova streets in Vancouver. The *Cassiar* became such a part of their life they incorporated it in a ditty:

Vancouver,

CPR,

Tommy Roberts,

Cassiar.

Above: Union vessels often overnighted at Lund, which was dominated by Charles Thulin's Hotel (centre).
Left: Of the *Cassiar* an observer once quipped, "She sat on the water with the easy grace of a stovepipe hat on a drunk's head."

As the primary mode of transportation between the city and the camps, the *Cassiar* acted as a shock absorber of sorts. Loggers were allowed to wear their caulk boots aboard (even to bed, if they wished) but were in turn asked to respect, as one writer puts it, the Union company's efforts at "civility" (i.e. they weren't supposed to pitch overboard the well-mannered stewards who strode the decks before each meal, banging a gong and announcing in singsong: "First call to lunch...").

For loggers, the best feature of the *Cassiar* was the bar—a small but well-stocked room which often wafted heavy fumes of unwashed armpits and wet wool Stanfields. The trouble with the bar was that marine law dictated it could only be open while the ship was in motion. To get around this regulation ingenious camps installed two floats. The *Cassiar* would dock at one float, everybody would pile aboard, and the ship would cast off for the other float, one hundred yards away. At drinking speed the *Cassiar* could take a half hour to traverse the distance.

Strong men and booze inevitably resulted in conflagrations. When things got too unruly aboard the *Cassiar*, the job of dealing with these loggers fell to the ship's mates. The most famous of these was Arthur Jarvis, a blue-eyed Irishman from Philadelphia. Jarvis was known as the "Black Mate," for his shock of black hair. He was the ship's designated bouncer. For this task he was equipped admirably, having trained as a boxer and possessing fists as hard as hemlock. When the *Cassiar* was slowed by a logger who suddenly had second thoughts and refused to get on board, Jarvis would hustle him into a makeshift corral at a dock and hammer sense into him. When dealing with a man too drunk to fight, Jarvis used the classic seat-of-the-pants-and-collar grip to toss him into the on-board jail.

Jarvis's reputation was legendized further by an incident that occurred in the early days of the *Cassiar*'s history. The ship was at Van Anda on Texada Island, unloading twenty pigs for Chow Dan, a local merchant. Some pigs were black, some were white. When one of the white pigs made a scrambling escape over the side, the Black Mate hurled himself

Like its corporate foster parent, the Union Steamship Co. of New Zealand, the Union Steamship Co. of BC believed passengers should be treated as royally as possible. Here a steward announces mealtime with a gong.

Three Union deckhands in the tradition of the Black Mate. It wasn't unheard of for Union ships to make unscheduled stops to call in police to subdue partying loggers.

after it. As any Union man who's wrestled a pig knows (and there were many), it is a miserable task even in broad daylight. But this was in the dark of night. A churning and sputtering and hurling about of arms and legs and pig's feet ensued; there was plenty of vigorous splashing, followed by some fantastically foul language. The Black Mate emerged— to the everlasting wonder of Union Steamship men since—lugging one squealing *black* pig.

For isolated communities like Sayward, the *Cassiar* was the only regular contact with the outside world.

In later years, Bill Hodgson took over from Jarvis. Hodgson had red hair and was called the "Red Mate." Like Jarvis, he knew more about knocking out teeth than he did about rigging snotters and Turk's heads.

Occasionally it was the *Cassiar*'s crew that was the source of trouble. Before each trip, crew were obliged to sign a form that included a list of "Regulations to Maintain Discipline." Among the twenty-two listed offences (and punishments):

• Insolence or contemptuous language or behaviour towards the Master of any Mate. (Punishment: One Day's Pay.)
• Striking or assaulting any person on board or belonging to the ship. (Two Day's Pay.)
• Quarrelling or provoking a quarrel. (One Day's Pay.)
• Swearing or using improper language. (One Day's Pay.)
• Bringing or having on board spirituous liquors. (Three Day's Pay.)
• Interrupting Divine Service by indecorous conduct. (One Day's Pay.)
• Not being cleaned, shaved, and washed on Sundays. (One Day's Pay.)
• Drunkenness. First offense. (Two Day's half allowance of provisions.)
• Ditto. Second offence. (Two Day's Pay.)
• Carrying a sheath-knife. (One Day's Pay.)

The *Cassiar*'s trip up-coast from Vancouver was considerably different than its run down-coast. The ship was quieter, and the loggers, many of them broke and suffering hangovers from a boozy holiday in the city, were eager to get back to work. Logger Jim Mackay once described the up-coast trip:

"When the camps got going you'd drag your ass down to the Union Steamships dock, get on the Cassiar, *get your stateroom and all, snoop around and see if there was any babes on board, maybe get together in someone's room for a hair of the dog, trade gossip about which guys were going to which camp up the line. Well, before you know it, the boat's comin' let's say into Lasqueti Island. You'd all go out and hang over the rail, everybody on the island'd be there on the dock, there'd always be someone you'd know. Charlie Klein'd be tryin' to talk you into gettin' off to help him for a couple of weeks, women'd be screamin'*

scandal back and forth, some gyppo maybe would be there catchin' freight and guys up on the boat would be after him about work, he'd be sayin', well, have you ever run a Skagit, yup, well—last-minute negotiations, the skipper'd be listening from the bridge to see which way it went, maybe hold the boat a bit, people'd be stumbling along still yappin' as the boat eased back, shouting and waving—and this would go on all the way up the line....That kinda kept things together, you see. The coast in them days was like a buncha people along a street seeing each other all the time on the way by."

In all the years of squirming in and out of bays and channels, the *Cassiar* had only one serious mishap. This was on August 16, 1917. It was 2:30 a.m. and the *Cassiar* was steaming full speed under the control of pilot Jock Robertson when it piled onto a rock on Privett Island, in Simoom Sound, near Gilford Island. Privett Island is shaped like a half-moon and as soon as the *Cassiar* hit, Robertson put it in full speed astern and backed it to the other side of the bay.

The *Cassiar*'s flexible wooden hull absorbed all but the heaviest of collisions, like the one in Simoon Sound in 1917. Salvage cost was approximately $30,000.

Although it was dark, there was virtually no panic among the passengers. There was one woman aboard, a Mrs. Johnstone, bound for the Charles Creek Cannery. Lifeboats were readied and, while loggers and crew waited, Mrs. Johnstone climbed into one of them and sat down regally. Then everyone else piled in and the crew rowed the passengers to a nearby settlement.

When daylight came the *Cassiar* was found to be badly damaged. At high tide only the tip of its bow was visible. The salvagers pulled it off so it was completely submerged. Then, while it was submerged, they turned the wreck around and pulled it gradually up on the beach, patching holes as they appeared. It was then towed to Vancouver by the tug, *Salvor*. On the voyage down, the chief engineer stayed aboard to keep the pumps going. The worst part of the trip, he later recalled, was walking over the swarms of drowned rats that littered the alleyways and decks.

Once repaired, the *Cassiar* resumed sailing and worked for another six years. By the time it was retired, in 1923, it had made over 1730 voyages, averaging 500 miles each, for a total of 865,000 miles.

Among routes the Union company opened in the first years of the century, none was more important than the one to Prince Rupert and the canneries of the Skeena and Nass Rivers. This run began in 1906, when the Union ship *Camosun*, under Capt. Frank "Fog Wizard" Saunders, first called with a few passengers and supplies. Tuck's Inlet, as it was known to pioneers, had just been chosen over nearby Port Essington as terminus for the country's second transcontinental railway, the Grand Trunk Pacific. Full of promise, but little else, the town was a collection of surveyors' tents linked by wobbly boardwalks.

The *Camosun* was designed specifically for the northern route. A combination freighter/passenger ship, it was heavy enough to withstand the rigours of crossing Queen Charlotte Sound, yet small enough to squeeze into canneries and small logging camps. It never did achieve the status of the *Cassiar*, but to those up-coast residents it served, the company never had a better ship.

The *Camosun* was built to meet competition to north coast areas from Canadian Pacific's *Princess Victoria*, and the Boscowitz Company's *Vadso* and *Venture*.

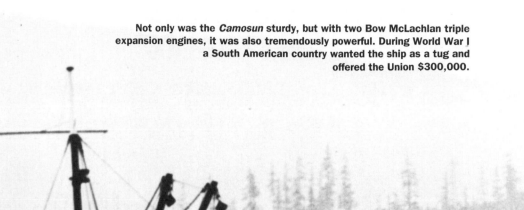

Not only was the *Camosun* sturdy, but with two Bow McLachlan triple expansion engines, it was also tremendously powerful. During World War I a South American country wanted the ship as a tug and offered the Union $300,000.

Above: The *Camosun*'s double bottom proved an invaluable feature in unsurveyed areas such as early Prince Rupert Harbour, where the *Camosun* ran aground in July 1906.

Right: Canneries were often built without consideration of the ships that had to serve them.

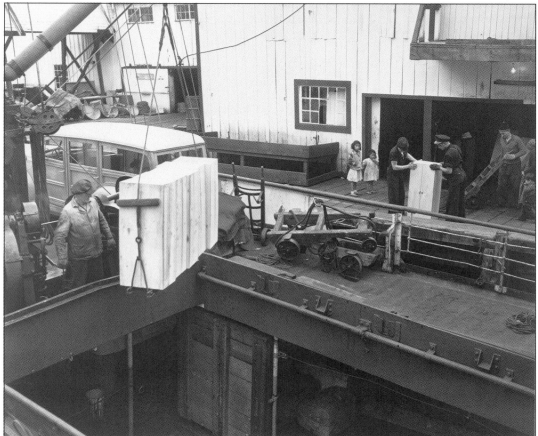

Above: Loading canned salmon at Butedale.

Right: Native families heading for the canneries aboard the *Camosun*. Passenger limits were often ignored in the rush to get seasonal workers upcoast.

In the years after 1906, the *Camosun* lugged every imaginable item into Prince Rupert, including dirt. Living on rock, the town's residents often requested Union boats bring good Fraser Valley topsoil to help their vegetable gardens. The *Camosun* also carried cattle, that in turn were slaughtered to feed railway construction crews. These animals were transported on deck. On one occasion, fifty nervous head staged an impromptu on-deck stampede, forcing the crew to take to the rigging.

Mostly, though, the *Camosun*, and the other ships that joined it on the northern runs, carried salmon. The golden age of the canning industry was just beginning and long-legged canneries were springing up in Smith's Inlet, Rivers Inlet and on the Skeena and Nass Rivers. As they did, the Union company moved quickly to capture their business. Starting in the first decade and continuing through the twenties, thirties and into the forties, Union steamers left Vancouver in the summer season loaded to the Plimsoll line with livestock, produce, machinery and coal, and wallowed back with huge loads of canned salmon.

For Union crews on the up-coast cannery route, the season started with preparing the ship for the thousands of Chinese workers who manned the canneries. This involved building hundreds of bunks in the second class section. The bunks consisted of stanchions and planks—no mattress. (A worker provided his own mattress, a straw mat known as a "donkey's breakfast.") Crates of chickens and bok choy littered the decks while below, workers smoked opium. Policy at the time was to jam as many in as possible and it wasn't unheard of to have five hundred people on a ship licensed for two hundred and eighty.

The *Camosun* wheeling away from the Campbell River dock, about 1907.

The difficult task of navigating shallow inlets and river estuaries attracted onlookers.

One of the biggest challenges for Union captains was getting ships into the canneries on the Skeena and Nass rivers. There were often only one or two channels deep enough to accommodate Union vessels, and these shifted as the rivers slowly changed course. It wasn't uncommon for skippers to "feel" their way in, steering the ship by the sound of sand scraping against the hull. Then, once they were docked at a cannery, there was the problem of tides. A heavily loaded ship could get out of the river only at high tide. The trick was to get in, service several canneries, then get out before the tide dropped and left the ship marooned.

Complicating all this were the fishing boats that littered the estuaries of the rivers. On the Skeena alone there were thirteen to fourteen canneries, each operating from 65 to 125 small fish boats. These small boats were towed out by a steam tender in the

Above: The *Camosun* at Margaret Bay, between Smith and Boswell Inlets. Small fishing vessels, like those in foreground, made navigation difficult for larger Union ships.

Left: Occasional groundings were the inevitable result of running a ship like the *Camosun*, which had a 17.9' draft, among shoals and sandbars.

evening and retrieved in the morning. During the night they let out their gillnets, which strung across the river like a maze. For a Union boat confined to a few channels, the only option was to steam right through. The ship would give four long blasts—code, as one captain put it, for "I'm coming!" Then, when the ship was over the nets, they'd cut the engine. That way the net would pass under the hull and, with luck, miss the propeller.

An immensely powerful ship, the *Camosun* set Union records for the Vancouver to Prince Rupert run several times, the fastest being forty-three hours, forty-six minutes. By 1935, however, the ship was worn out. The reputable *Camosun* was anchored in Bedwell Bay, then towed to Japan for scrapping.

Chapter Three

1908-1914: Sinking of the Cheslakee

Sea gull, sea gull, sit on the sand,
It's never good weather when you're on the land.
Traditional seaman's jingle

Opposite:
A ship with a
checkered history. The
***Cheakamus* steaming**
out of Vancouver.

Early on the morning of July 21, 1908, a single-funnel steamer nosed its way out of the Strait of Georgia, through the First Narrows and alongside the Union dock. Heavy hemp lines were heaved dockside and Capt. Charles Polkinghorne rang down for "stop." The ship had just finished a ninety-day voyage from the dockyards of the Ailsa Shipbuilding Co. in Troon, Scotland, around the Horn and up the west coast, stopping only twice—at Buenos Aires and San Francisco—for coal.

The name on the side of the ship was the *Cariboo*, but due to a mix-up with another vessel of the same name operating on the Great Lakes, that was changed within days to *Cowichan*. The SS *Cowichan* was the first of several ships the Union company acquired in the years before World War One. These ships were built in the expectation of an economic boom, especially in the north, where rumours abounded about a new contract awarded for another leg of the Grand Trunk Railway.

Unlike earlier Union vessels, the *Cowichan* was designed specifically for the BC coast. The bridge was moved forward and the wheelhouse enlarged to enable the navigator and quartermaster to see over the bow when docking. It also had two engines which made it more manoeuvrable in small coves and passes.

The *Cowichan* was equipped to handle 125–150 tons of general cargo, and was licensed for 165 passengers, who were put up in stylish accommodations. A Vancouver *Province* article gushed the virtues of the new craft: "This new steamer is more than has been

The *Cariboo*, later *Cowichan*, leaving Troon, Scotland, for Vancouver, Spring 1908.

Right: The *Cowichan* was converted from coal to oil in 1912. The high cost of the changeover was more than offset by savings in operating costs.

modestly claimed for her by the owners. The expense of her interior must have been enormous for a vessel of her size and purpose. The woodwork is of the most uniform grain English white oak and in that respect eclipses any other ships coming here.

"One good feature is the separation of the different classes. A First Class passenger gets what he pays for, including spaciousness and exclusiveness. There is little chance for annoyance by loud talking and the provision made for ladies in the aftermusic room is excellent.

Above: The company head office at the foot of Carrall St.

Left: The Union dock in Vancouver. Union officials discovered it best to schedule departures for logging camp routes in the mornings, before local bars and hotels opened.

On time trials in Belfast the *Chelohsin* exceeded 14 knots, though normal cruising speed was 12.5 knots. The captain who brought her across the Atlantic claimed "She was like a racing yacht."

"The loggers have quarters all to themselves. They are good and commodious and they get full value for lower fare.

"There is a special cabin for Indians and Klo-oches, another for Chinese and Japs.

"The dining room is first class and the kitchen is superior in character and equipment."

The *Cowichan* made its first trip, to Van Anda and Campbell River, under veteran Union navigator—he was a captain at age twenty-one—Charles Moody. Then the ship was put on the logging runs, leaving Union docks Mondays and Wednesdays. Saturdays and holidays were for excursions. A popular, fast ship, it was soon dubbed "the Cow."

Three years later, on December 28, 1911, another new Union vessel pulled into Vancouver. This was the SS *Chelohsin*. The *Chelohsin* had been built by the Dublin Dockyard Company for approximately $140,500. It was a twin screw vessel of 1134 gross tons. The day after the *Chelohsin* arrived, the *Vancouver Daily News-Advertiser* announced: "Old timers who were at the wharf to welcome the vessel said that she was one of the smartest looking vessels they had ever seen. The *Chelohsin* is very beamy, but with her racing lines and her sheer, loses the appearance of width....Her passenger accommodation is the equal of any vessel in the coastwise business. The *Chelohsin* embraces many ideas which will commend her to travellers on this coast."

Known to many as the "Logger's Hearse," the *Chelohsin* first served the northern runs, then was placed on the logging camp routes.

The *Chelohsin* at Beaver Creek, in Loughborough Inlet.

The *Chelohsin*, known as the "Charlie Olsen," was on Union logging runs for years. Among early captains was Jack Edwards, a former sailor who maintained his muscular physique by taking an axe into the nearby woods to chop trees during layovers in Powell River.

Like the *Cassiar*, the *Chelohsin* became an integral part of logging life on the coast. Unlike the *Cassiar*, however, it didn't have a Red Mate or Black Mate to maintain discipline. One crewman improvised a billy club made from wire rope to keep order. One of the first loggers to receive this treatment was a Swedish man caught tearing the ship apart, looking for a drink. The purser asked the second mate to invite this logger up to his cabin for a drink. The plan was that when the logger walked into the mate's cabin, the purser would clobber him over the head. "Wait a minute," said the mate, "what are you going to hit him with 'cause I'll be the guy inviting him out for the drink and I'll be the guy he'll be looking for." The purser showed him the wire billy. The mate said, "That'll fix him."

When the second mate made his pitch to the logger; as he later recalled, the Swede answered with "Ya, ya, ya!" He led the man up to his cabin, and when the Swede stepped in, the purser let him have it on the head—twice. The Swede collapsed like a rotten snag.

"Did you have to hit him that hard?" asked the mate. "You didn't have to kill the bastard, did you?"

The purser was unrepentant. "He's not dead," he said. "You can't kill a Swede that way."

As part of the fleet upgrading that included the purchase of the *Cowichan* and *Chelohsin*, company officials had planned to build an even larger vessel to use on the up-coast run. But this plan was altered by the announcement in 1909 that the Grand Trunk Railway was going into the steamer business. Union ships on the northern run already had competition from the Canadian Pacific's *Princess Beatrice* and *Princess May*, as well as

The *Cowichan* outbound off Prospect Point, Vancouver.

Northern Steamship's *Petriana*. The Grand Trunk first went into service with a clunky old steamer, the *Bruno*, but obviously had great things in mind as it ordered two stupendous 310-foot liners, the *Prince Rupert* and the *Prince George*.

As a result the Union company toned down its plans and opted to build a more modest vessel. This seemed wise at the time, although it eventually figured in the worst disaster in Union history.

The vessel was the SS *Cheslakee*. The hull and main deck of the *Cheslakee* were built in 1910 at the Dublin Dockyard and towed to Belfast, where triple expansion engines built by MacColl & Co. were added. It was then readied for the trip to Vancouver, where the rest of the superstructure was to be completed.

The *Cheslakee* departed Belfast on June 29, amid a chaotic scene, a perverse foreshadowing of what was to come several years later. The calamity started June 28 with a huge party that left Capt. J.W. Starkey, a "specialist" in new ship delivery, out of commission for several days. Then, minutes before the ship was due to cast off, the cook, a small man five feet tall, got into an argument with his wife. She had come down to see her husband off on the long voyage. Both were apparently very drunk. The cook kissed his wife, boarded the ship, then returned, wobbling down the narrow gangplank, to say farewell again. Somehow an argument developed. There were heated words, and the cook punched his wife. She punched him back. He stalked off, weaving his way up the gangplank. In a few minutes the cook was overcome with remorse and teetered down the gangplank and the scene repeated itself. Finally, the *Cheslakee* managed to cast off. As it steamed out of the harbour it passed two enormous liners under construction. Every man working on the two big liners left his post to watch the *Cheslakee* steam around the harbour and off on her long journey. The liners were the *Titanic* and the *Olympic*.

On arrival in Vancouver the cook disappeared. Several days later he showed up at the company's office with a sailfish tucked under his arm, ready for mounting. As he

The CPR's enormous Pier D dominated the Vancouver waterfront. Canadian Pacific's Princess ships generally served larger southern centres, while small coastal routes were left to the Union.

The ill-fated and ill-designed *Cheslakee* at a float in Lewis Channel. Addition of an overheavy superstructure left the vessel with a noticeable list.

explained to the perplexed staff, it was "a herring to catch a mackerel," meaning a bribe to secure his job.

In Vancouver, a contract for completing the *Cheslakee*'s superstructure was awarded to Wallace's Shipyard at North Vancouver. Twenty-three first class cabins were added, providing fifty-six berths and a small lounge. The *Cheslakee* was granted a BC Coast licence for 148 passengers. Her dining salon provided thirty seats; her freight capacity was 120 tons.

On its voyage to Vancouver, the *Cheslakee* had performed well in heavy seas. "Varying kinds of weather were struck but in the worst of the storms the vessel took the seas easily and shipped no water," the captain observed. "The crew that brought her round the Horn were all impressed by the seaworthiness of the craft." On its first trip out after refit, however, the *Cheslakee* rolled and swayed like a harpooned whale. It had a permanent list. Later, while passing through Surge Narrows, it keeled over at such an angle the crew thought it might capsize. Sooner or later, more than one local mariner observed, that ship would get into serious trouble.

At 8:45 p.m. Monday, January 6, 1913, the *Cheslakee* steamed out of Vancouver, heading up-coast—the first scheduled stop to be Van Anda, near the north end of Texada Island—and carrying ninety-seven passengers and forty-five tons of cargo. The captain was John Cockle. The sea was building with a rising wind when the steamer docked at Van Anda at 3:25 a.m. to let off eight passengers and several boards of freight. The *Cheslakee* departed twenty minutes later. By this time the squall had turned into a storm blowing ESE. A mile and a half on its way to Powell River, the *Cheslakee* was hit by a gust estimated at 65 mph. The ship took two heavy seas and listed to port 25 degrees, breaking cargo loose.

First officer Robert Wilson cranked the ship's helm to port, hoping the force of the gale would counter the list. Turning back for Van Anda, he called for Captain Cockle. As the *Cheslakee* neared the dock at Van Anda, its fires were extinguished, lights went out and it was forced to make a starboard landing in utter darkness. Below decks, the engineer reported water pouring in through the ash chute, which was now below the surface. The pumps were started but they soon became choked with coal dust.

As soon as the *Cheslakee* was secured, gangplanks were run out. It was a calamitous situation, as described by a passenger: "Lights were out almost as soon as the vessel reached the wharf, as water had drowned out the fires....[T]he officers acted with cool precision and there was practically no panic among the passengers. [The officers] did not tell the passengers what had happened but ordered them to get off as quickly as possible....The boat was sinking rapidly, in fact one could feel the deck falling beneath one's feet and the lower she sank the further away from the wharf she tilted."

Left: The captain of the *Cheslakee* had wanted to make a port landing, so the vessel would settle onto the dock, but was prevented from doing so when water extinguished the engine fires.

Below and bottom: The sinking and subsequent salvage of the *Cheslakee* were being recalled on Texada Island 80 years later.

Suddenly, with the *Cheslakee* listing away from the dock, the gangplank crashed into the water, taking with it several passengers, who were rescued. A longer gangplank was put out. Inside, crew struggled in the dark to guide passengers out. Captain Cockle discovered three men stuck in the forward smoking room. Hanging to an entrance with both hands, he extended himself full length and one by one, the men scrambled over his body to safety.

Within five minutes of coming alongside the dock the *Cheslakee*'s forward lines broke. The ship reeled over, dropping several passengers off the gangplank into the water. The last to leave were the purser, a Chinese cook, and two Japanese passengers, who jumped overboard. The cook vanished after hitting the wintery water. Eighty-three passengers and crew made it ashore, but six passengers and one crew didn't. As the *Cheslakee* flooded, she levelled off and sunk at the dock with only the stack and the top of her pilot-house showing.

Among those still trapped inside were two loggers, Samuel Courtney and John Hartlin. Hartlin was smaller than Courtney, and figured he might manage to squeeze out a porthole. The two men shook hands, then Hartlin took his fist and, pounding it to a bloody pulp, was able to shatter the window. Before Hartlin left, Courtney said: "I've cursed this ship from the first time I rode on it and now I've got to die on it." Hartlin squeezed out and swam to safety.

That night, the death toll on the *Cheslakee* could not be calculated. But the next morning the ship began giving up its victims. The cook's body was found with a life jacket tangled around his legs. A drowned baby was found on deck, tucked among bales of hay. A lifeboat destroyed a stateroom window and the body of a woman floated out, her loose hair wafting in the water. She was one of two teachers drowned in the accident—Mrs. Simpson and Miss M. Pepper—whose fatal modesty prevented them from appearing in public dressed only in nightgowns. When everyone was accounted for, the death toll was seven. This accident was the only one in the company's history involving loss of life on a Union passenger ship.

Above: The *Salvor*, alongside the sunken *Cheslakee* on the evening of January 6, 1913.

A marine inquiry confirmed what passengers and crew had contended for years. The *Cheslakee* was unstable. And the cause of this, surmised inquiry officials, was the addition of the superstructure, which, they noted, was "heavier than allowed for by the designer." What

The *Cheakamus*, formerly the *Cheslakee*, at Valdez Island. After the Van Anda accident the hull was cut in half and twenty feet added—the first time this method was used on the BC coast.

the inquiry was unable to confirm, however, was the suspicion of locals that there were more than seven deaths aboard the *Cheslakee*. According to longtime Texada resident Bill Young, divers working on the sunken *Cheslakee* claimed there were eleven loggers on board. They were in the hold and, as was often the case, not recorded on the ship's passenger list. Furthermore, Young claimed he was acquainted with a local resident named Brandy—"got his name honestly"—who accompanied the *Cheslakee* down to Vancouver, and who said they flushed the loggers at sea while passing Stillwater and Jervis Inlet.

The task of raising the *Cheslakee* was awarded to the BC Salvage Company, which sent the SS *Salvor* to Van Anda. It was a huge event on Texada—in part because of the opportunities for looting. A looted ten-gallon keg of beer bounced nearly all over the island before someone put a bung in it. Sports fishermen found flotsam from the wreck, including several crates containing a gallon of rye whiskey and a gallon of pickles. These, according to one resident at the time, made for an epically good fishing trip. Several weeks after the sinking, the *Cheslakee* was raised, pumped and taken to Vancouver drydock. It was cut in half, twenty feet were added, and it was relaunched as the SS *Cheakamus*.

A completely different ship, the *Cheakamus* was stable in heavy seas and a favourite of regular passengers. It worked for the Union until 1941, when the ghost-ridden steamer was sold to the US Army Transport Service for $75,000.

F VALDEZ ISLAND B C

Chapter Four

1914-1920:
World War One

The efficiency of a steamship consists not so much in her courage as in the power she carries within herself.
It beats and throbs like a pulsating heart within her iron ribs, and when it stops, the steamer, whose life is not so much a
contest as the disdainful ignoring of the sea, sickens and dies upon the waves.

Joseph Conrad, The Mirror of the Sea, 1923

The Union's shipbuilding spree came to an end with the declaration of war in 1914. The economy, already sluggish, became virtually stagnant. Provincial lumber production, over 1 billion board feet in 1913, plummeted to 607 million board feet a year later. Camps closed down, settlers packed up. Businesses in general suffered as thousands of men trundled off to the battlefields of Europe.

Early in 1914, several months before the outbreak of war, a rumour drifted into conversations along the Vancouver waterfront. German warships, it was said, were lurking off the coast. Exactly how many depended on the version of the rumour being recounted. Two. Three. Five. Some claimed there was an entire German Pacific Squadron out there, just waiting for the command to go into action against unarmed, unsuspecting merchant vessels. With coastal defences consisting of nothing more than the HMCS *Rainbow*, a rusting, obsolete cruiser, sailors didn't need a degree in naval strategy to imagine the havoc such a force could inflict.

For the Union, the rumour was as close as it would get to involvement in World War One; for two men associated with the company, the rumour would have a very direct impact on their lives. It propelled Barney Johnson, a prewar Union captain, and Harry McLean, a postwar company captain, into one of the more bizarre episodes in the war—the purchase, by the Province of British Columbia, of two submarines, the infamous HMCS *CC 1* and the HMCS *CC 2*.

These submarines were bought just hours after the declaration of war, on August 4, 1914, on orders of Premier Richard McBride. McBride had heard the talk about

Opposite:
Used primarily on day trips, the *Capilano* had a loyal following among residents of Howe Sound and the Sunshine Coast.

German warships and, desperate for a way to defend the coast, arranged for the purchase of the two vessels from the Electric Boat Co. The *Iquique* and *Antofagasta* had been built for the Chilean navy, but were lying idle in Seattle because the Chilean navy claimed they were defective. McBride picked up the two for $1,150,000.

The story of these pontoon-like craft is, as marine historian Norman Hacking has said, something straight out of Gilbert and Sullivan's "HMS *Pinafore*." Just hours after being purchased, in an at-sea deal five miles southeast of Trial Island, near Victoria, they were almost blown out of the water by Canadian gunners, who mistook them for the enemy. Then it was discovered the Chileans were right, the subs were defective. Furthermore, virtually no one knew how to navigate a submarine, so a hastily assembled crew practised descending with the craft while still tied to the docks at Esquimalt. When the subs finally went to sea, it was to do nothing less critical than blasting off dummy torpedoes (while above water) at Dallas Road beach.

Johnson was pilot aboard one of the submarines. An experienced coastal navigator, he had worked for the Union company from 1898 to 1906, serving as master of the *Capilano*, *Comox* and *Camosun*. He was twenty-two when given the first of these commands and dubbed the "Boy Captain" by up-coast residents. McLean, a regular crew member aboard the subs, still had his Union days ahead of him. He was to be with the company from 1920 to 1953, the last thirteen years as master aboard various vessels.

From the start, McLean and Johnson saw the subs were a farce and sought ways to transfer off. Johnson was given command of another sub overseas eventually, and with HM Submarine *H8* he had a distinguished war career. On one occasion the *H8* struck a mine off Holland and Johnson had to reverse one hundred miles back to base in England. For this, he was awarded the DSO.

Chief officer (later Captain) Harry McLean

Above: Unarmed and confined to narrow waterways, Union vessels would have been easy targets for German warships.

Left: BC's submarines, the *CC 1* and *CC 2*. The *CC 1* is alongside the dock.

McLean's break from the *CC 1* and *CC 2* was cleaner. He left the navy altogether, transferring to the army. He went overseas and was badly gassed while fighting in the trenches. McLean lost his vision for three years and, despite forty-two operations, many while he was with the Union company, he never regained his sense of smell.

Shadowy German battleships or not, Union schedules had to be maintained during the war. Not only were up-coast communities totally dependent on vessels such as the *Camosun*, *Cowichan*, *Cassiar* and *Chelohsin*, but the company was obliged to keep schedules

Below: The *Camosun* ran aground on Digby Island, outside Prince Rupert Harbour, on March 7, 1916. Seventeen passengers and over 100 tons of coal and wartime supplies had to be lightened off before the ship was pulled free, on March 17.

if it was to receive a government mail subsidy, which it needed to offset losses on routes into uneconomical areas.

During the company's first two decades, the biggest problem facing Union vessels was getting from A to B. Rocks and reefs had to be charted, currents noted, and shortest, safest routes between ports logged. By 1914, however, the major routes were known, and the problem became one of keeping ships running day after day. This was the job of the engine room crew.

Like deck crews and stewards, engine room crews had their own hierarchy. In the years before 1910, when most Union ships burned coal, the lowliest positions in the engine room were the trimmers and stokers, positions often filled by Japanese and Chinese workers. Trimmers grunted coal from dark, dusty bunkers to the boilers; stokers shovelled the coal into the boilers and kept the coal burning as cleanly as possible. The first job broke backs; the second, with constant exposure to the hot blast of the boilers, cooked men alive.

On Union ships, the stoker's job was complicated by the fact that the Vancouver Island coal they were burning was of such poor quality, it tended to form clinkers, which in turn checked the fire. This added to the inherent misery of the job, because stokers were constantly having to break the clinkers from the furnace bars.

The shift from coal to oil, accomplished in the years just before World War One, was made for several reasons. Engines on oil-fired steamers were more responsive than those fired by coal, meaning navigators had an easier time docking. Furthermore, they needed less maintenance and lasted longer; and without the bulk of coal, vessels could carry more cargo. Most importantly, at least from the company's point of view, oil-fired engines reduced labour. On an oil-burning ship, one man could do the work of eighteen firemen and between six and nine trimmers.

Still, using oil required skill. The trick with oil was to get the right amount

When making repairs engineers had to make do with what they could find or manufacture aboard.

on a fire. Put too much on and the effect was similar to dousing a bonfire with gas: much of it disappeared up the stack in a filthy black cloud. Too little fuel, on the other hand, and pressure dropped, the vessel lost power, and the responsible engineer was subjected to reams of filthy language from the captain.

Lording over the engine room and its staff was the chief engineer. Technically, the chief engineer ranked just below the captain in a ship's hierarchy; in reality, most chief engineers thought of themselves a notch above masters, whose job, it seemed to engineers, was to strut around the deck with female passengers.

Working day after day, year after year in the engine room, many engineers developed an intuitive skill with machinery, and were able to monitor the bearing temperatures, head pressures and a host of other mechanical vital signs with a single sniff of the engine room air. One chief engineer on the *Chelohsin*, for example, could notice minute fluctuations in the engine revolutions while reading his morning paper, which he usually did sprawled on an old car seat he had wedged into the engine room.

Known to many as "the Chief," Paddy Farina was synonymous with the wooden-hulled *Capilano II*.

Junior engineers would ease the throttle ahead slightly while the chief was buried in the sports section. Several minutes later, inevitably, a corner of the paper would drop, and the chief could be seen with his head cocked to one side, dog-like, studying the thump, thump, thump of the *Chelohsin*'s engine. Then he'd adjust the throttle back to its proper position.

Many chief engineers also developed an almost maniacal affinity for their charges. The prime example on Union ships was a pear-faced Englishman named Paddy Farina. Farina started working for the Union company in 1910, first as second engineer on the *Camosun*, then on the *Comox*, where he was chief engineer. In 1919, he joined a ship he was to stay on for thirty years, the SS *Capilano II*.

Built of seasoned Douglas fir, the *Capilano II* was designed to serve ports near Vancouver, licensed to carry 350 passengers from May to September and 150 during the rest of the year. It was powered by two inverted direct-acting, triple expansion, NHP 51 engines, that had been taken out of the steamer *Washington*, bought a year earlier from a Seattle firm for $45,000. At the time, these engines were regarded as the best on the coast for their size.

Paddy was a man of habits. He attributed his own solid health to a daily lunch of sliced tomatoes and virgin olive oil. The health of his engines aboard the *Capilano II* he attributed to a daily shining. They were shined and shined, and shined again. They were the cleanest in the fleet. Farina would do anything to ensure their good performance. Even in the heat of summer, when engine rooms turned into fumy ovens, he forbade other engine room staff to open doors or hatches. The cool air, he lectured, didn't make for proper combustion.

The hull of the *Capilano II* was built by BC Marine for $70,000. It was launched at 2 p.m., Saturday December 20, 1919. A newspaper of the time reported, "The little craft slipped down the ways in perfect style."

Thick black smoke was usually the result of poor fuel or a cool engine.

With a maximum speed of 13.5 knots and capacity for 350 passengers, the *Capilano II* was an ideal day-boat for small excursions. It ran three times a week to Selma Park, with stops at Roberts Creek and Wilson Creek; on Sundays the trip included Halfmoon Bay (often called Redrooffs) and Buccaneer Bay on Thormanby Island. The ship's clean appearance suggests the photo was taken soon after launching.

Farina developed an affection for the *Capilano* that astonished even other Union engineers. Jimmy Butterfield, a Vancouver newspaper columnist at the time, took a trip on the *Capilano* and later wrote a story about the journey, referring to the *Capilano* as a "pot-bellied" and "fussy" little boat that only put into sawmills, squatters' villages and other backwater settlements. One year later, Butterfield reboarded the *Capilano*. He was greeted by Farina who, Butterfield said, had his "prognathous jaw ajar."

"Are you called Butterfield?" asked Farina.

Butterfield said he was afraid so.

Farina took a step closer. "Come here," he said, "I'm going to kill you."

Farina then described how he had been keeping a dull axe especially for the purpose "since you called this packet a pot-bellied something or other." Recalling the event later, Butterfield said Farina "seemed to mean it." In the end, the conflict was resolved peacefully, Butterfield having to crack a bottle of good Scotch to pacify the overheated engineer.

Engineers were also responsible for getting Union vessels going when they broke down away from port. In the company's early days this meant improvising under some very adverse conditions.

In April 1917, while attempting to deliver supplies to the Drumlummon Mine in Douglas Channel, the Union's SS *Coquitlam* was caught in the rush of an incoming tide. The mine was located on a long and shallow bay, and the current pushed the ship with such force that it was, according to first mate John Muir, "slashed" on a nearby rock cliff. The impact popped rivets and badly rattled the crew. The full extent of the damage wasn't suspected until some time later, when the *Coquitlam* began to list; as the ship lumbered northward, the list increased. An officer was sent to investigate. He discovered five feet of water in the hold, with more spewing in. Pumps were engaged and Capt. Neil Gray laid emergency plans.

Ship masters in those days, like bush pilots today, kept in their minds a list of coves, bays and beaches where a ship in distress might shelter quickly. If the situation was

Material for many pioneer enterprises was carried in the hold of the *Coquitlam*. In 1910 it hauled steel plate for the construction of the dam and pipeline at Ocean Falls.

bad enough, it wasn't unheard of to run a vessel ashore and make repairs. The trick to doing this was to take the ship in sideways, or "sidearm" on a high tide. That way the length of the hull was out of the water when the tide dropped.

The nearest such place Captain Gray could think of was a little shelving beach in Lowe Inlet, up Grenville Channel. It took the overburdened *Coquitlam* three hours to get there, the crew anxiously watching all the while as it sunk lower and lower in the water. When they arrived, the Captain misjudged and ran the ship ashore pointing almost straight in. The result was that the aft section of the ship, where it was holed, was still in the water.

As the crew could tell, the situation was terrible. Their holed vessel was poorly lodged on a beach in one of the most inhospitable sections of the coast. The area is surrounded by precipitous mountains whose stunted cedar forests are furrowed by avalanches and rock slides. It's the type of country that challenged the survival skills of the most hardy trappers and adventurers.

The job of fixing the *Coquitlam* fell to a young chief engineer, Freddie Smith. A lean man with a lopsided grin, Smith was in many ways the perfect engineer. He had been dealing with crises since his father, a member of the British House of Commons, got in with a gambling crowd, lost the family fortune, and died. That was in 1899; at the time Smith was eleven. He had been in private school but was forced to quit and take a job tending sheep in the Cotswold Hills for $1.25 a week. At fourteen, he was sent to Bristol to learn engineering.

One of Smith's friends at school had gone to sea and written warm accounts of the life. So, at nineteen, Smith went to Cardiff in south Wales and wandered the docks. He found a berth as fourth engineer on an old tramp steamer loading coal for the Black Sea. They sailed the same night Smith signed aboard. Smith said, "If the old ship was pushed and had the tide behind her she would do 5 knots. She had no generators, nothing but coal oil lamps and the food consisted of salted meat and hardtack biscuits that were full of maggots. The salted meat I think came from all the horses that had been killed in the Crimean War and had been pickled up, but you had to eat it because there was nothing else."

When they returned to England they landed at Swansea, Wales. The Captain said to Smith, "We're sailing in two days, go up to the shipping master and sign on again." Smith said, "Not me, I'm leaving this ship as soon as I can." So he went home to Gloucestershire, where his mother lived, and got a job in a factory doing piecework twelve hours a day. But family misfortune reigned, and when a younger brother contracted TB, his mother asked Smith to take him to the clear, wet air of British Columbia for recuperation.

But Smith had trouble finding work on the West Coast. He got a job on a tug working out of Vancouver; it tied up after one trip. A job in a Seattle shipyard lasted just six weeks. Next, he got a job as fourth engineer aboard the *Kingsley*, bound for Japan. Twenty days out in the Pacific and the *Kingsley* lost her rudder. Smith and the crew rigged up a jury rudder out of the ship's booms and set sail again. On the second night an enormous wave swept the jury rudder away. Without a wireless or light, they drifted until a French ship spotted them. It started to tow the *Kingsley* but had to cut them adrift because of a typhoon warning. They drifted again until a tug hauled them into Nagoya, Japan. They had finally reached their destination. But the man who arranged the whole deal had skipped out with all the money, so the crew never got paid. The skipper went to the British Consulate and they made it home via a destitute seamen's arrangement. In 1913 Smith joined Union Steamships.

On board the stranded *Coquitlam*, Smith faced two problems. First was

Top: Capt. Neil Gray was master of nine Union ships, including the *Coquitlam*, *Chilco* and, almost continuously from 1924-1937, the *Lady Cecilia*.

Above: Freddie Smith (centre) was the consummate chief engineer.

The *Coquitlam* was sold in May 1923. Union officials regretted the move as the handy vessel, renamed the *Bervin*, was to continue in coast service for many years.

time. He had a matter of hours before the tide came in and made it impossible to work. Any repairs were going to have to be done quickly. The second problem was tools. In a shipyard, where such repairs were normally done, workers had access to riveting guns, torches and overhead cranes. All Smith had to work with were a few hand tools and a dull axe.

The *Coquitlam*'s bent and buckled plates could be seen from the outside, but fixing them meant getting at them from the inside. This meant digging through a hold full of coal. When this was done, Smith and a deckhand chopped through the four-inch thick wood sheathing on the inside of the hull. This enabled Smith to squirm in. It was dirty, cold and dark, and there was no means of communicating with the crew. Using a plate from the stoke hold, Smith marked the place where the rivets were on the damaged hull plate. Then he pounded rivets out of the mangled metal, reinserted the plate, and reefed it tight with bolts. This pulled the careened hull plates flush. The tide came in, the *Coquitlam* floated off the beach, and the ship steamed into the calm waters of Grenville Channel, headed south for Vancouver.

Soon after the Douglas Channel accident, the *Coquitlam* and Freddie Smith were involved in another mishap. Coming across Queen Charlotte Sound on the way south, the *Coquitlam* had its propeller knocked off by a deadhead. After drifting for several hours, it was taken in tow by the Union ship *Venture* and beached at Alert Bay on tiny Cormorant Island, under the imposing brick hulk of the Indian residential school. Smith sent to Vancouver for another propeller but when it arrived it was discovered to be the wrong one. The problem was the key, the mechanism that holds the propeller on the tailshaft of the ship. It didn't fit. Faced with shipping the propeller back to be retooled or doing the job himself,

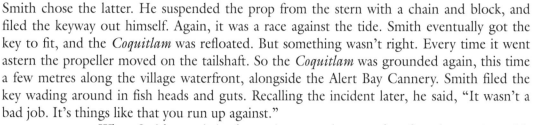

Smith chose the latter. He suspended the prop from the stern with a chain and block, and filed the keyway out himself. Again, it was a race against the tide. Smith eventually got the key to fit, and the *Coquitlam* was refloated. But something wasn't right. Every time it went astern the propeller moved on the tailshaft. So the *Coquitlam* was grounded again, this time a few metres along the village waterfront, alongside the Alert Bay Cannery. Smith filed the key wading around in fish heads and guts. Recalling the incident later, he said, "It wasn't a bad job. It's things like that you run up against."

When Smith wasn't in the engine room he was often found cavorting with female passengers. The combination of four stripes on his shoulder and a sonorous English accent had aphrodisiacal powers. An ample supply of Scotch in his room helped, too. Smith was one of those drinkers who threw the stopper away after opening a bottle. "This stuff won't keep, you know." On one occasion, after a night of drinking with a female passenger, he woke feeling so poorly he decided to have another drink. There was a glass on the bedside table with something in it so he opened the porthole and tossed the contents out. It turned out the contents were the woman's false teeth. The pain of Smith's hangover paled once the woman was done with him.

Although Smith was with the company until the 1950s, his greatest adventure came early in his career, in December 1919 when he was aboard the SS *Chilliwack*. The *Chilliwack* was a recent addition to the Union fleet, having been bought as the *Onyx* for $112,500.

The captain of the *Chilliwack* was C.B. Smith (no relation to Freddie), a tough square-rigger veteran with a washboard nose. The ship had just loaded seven hundred tons of wet ore concentrate at Surf Inlet, on the west side of Princess Royal Island. It was cold at the time of loading, and the concentrates froze. On the way south the concentrates thawed and, without hold dividers, turned into an unstable soup. Little by little, the *Chilliwack* listed to starboard, eventually going over 40 degrees.

Inside the effect of the list was nearly catastrophic. Water poured over the decks and down hatches and vent holes. Engine room firemen thought the ship was going over and ran from their stations. Only Smith and several other engineers were left to look after the boilers, working up to their knees in salt water because the pumps couldn't keep up with the incoming torrents. (Smith, in characteristic understatement, later remarked that a large amount of water was "admitted" into the engine room.) When the engines threatened to burn up for lack of lubricating oil, Smith doused them with buckets of salt water. There was no doubt about what would happen if they stopped: the *Chilliwack* would go down.

Eventually, Captain Smith was able to beach the disabled ship in a small cove on Price Island, off the southwest shore of Princess Royal Island. There it lay for three or four days while water was pumped out and bulkheads, made from logs hauled off the beach, inserted to stabilize the concentrate. During this time the engines had to be partly taken down and overhauled—no small feat in itself. The ship then continued to her destination.

Later, Freddie Smith received special thanks from Captain Smith for his work in helping save the *Chilliwack*. The captain confessed that while Smith was "sticking it out" during the *Chilliwack*'s worst moments, he had been on the bridge, strapped into a life jacket, ready to jump when the ship rolled.

After seven hard years with the Union company, the *Chilliwack* was sold to the Gosse Packing Co. for use as a floating cannery.

Chapter Five

1920-1925: Boat Day

We in the north living in isolation and wilderness of snow appreciate and bless this ship…and its Master.
Old and young live, wait and listen for that ship's shrill whistle which means it's our food supplies, mail, miners,
trappers, familiar faces returning back to their north abode. On boat days our children are restless at school, coaxing
their teacher to let them go down to the wharf to watch the ship come sliding in.
Letter to the editor, quoted in History of Bowen Island by Irene Howard

The Union company approached the 1920s with confidence by purging itself of several old vessels. The first to go was the SS *Comox*. Aging but still serviceable, it was sold, in the spring of 1920, to Vancouver Machinery Depot. Union officials thought the little ship was destined for the scrap heap, but VMD had other plans. They flipped the *Comox* to Alexander Woodside, a San Diego businessman. Captain Woodside stripped out the *Comox*'s Bow McLachlan engine, installed a newer model, then overhauled the rest of the ship. The MV *Alejandro*, as it was renamed, was soon in service on the Mexican coast. To coastal residents the affair seemed scandalous—akin to dumping a longtime employee just because he wasn't as sprightly as he had once been. A *Vancouver Sun* article summarized the feelings of many: "The Master of Ceremonies at [the *Alejandro*'s] launching should say— Ladies and Gentlemen, meet the motorship *Alejandro*, otherwise known as the *Comox*, dearly beloved of loggers and cannery hands on the British Columbia coast for thirty years."

Three years later, the company retired the venerable *Cassiar*. This time, at least, there seemed some justification for the move. Worn and battered, the *Cassiar* was no longer reliable enough for the increasing demands of the logging camp runs. It was purchased by a Puget Sound fishing company and given back its original name, *J.R. McDonald*. Six years later, it was resold and tied up on Lake Washington as a dance hall. The fate of the former *Cassiar* (the new name never took in BC) is unknown, but one rumour— the one Union employees liked to believe—is that before it faded from the scene it had one last fling at fame, as a set in the classic Charlie Chaplin movie, *The Gold Rush*.

The departure of these early mainstays of the Union fleet marked the company's transition into the busiest period of its history. The twenties didn't just roar on

Opposite:
A Union boat approaching Halfmoon Bay. Residents of small communities could tell who was on the bridge by the way the ship docked.

The *Cassiar*'s post-Union life continued long after it was sold. In 1935 it was lying in Lake Union, Washington, with "Bugge Fisheries" painted on the hull.

the coast, they bellowed. This was the heyday of the forest and mining industries. Union boats shipped pulp from Powell River, Ocean Falls and Swanson Bay. They shipped copper from Anyox and Surf Inlet. They brought supplies to the constellations of camps and settlements from Howe Sound right up the coast to the Skeena.

If a stamp is ever issued commemorating this era on the coast, it will depict a Union steamer tied to a jutting log wharf. The ship's winch is in action, lowering a pallet of goods to a small crowd of wool-clad men. On the bridge, the captain leans against the railing, chatting with an attentive woman below. Behind them, so faint as to be barely visible, a man on deck is surreptitiously passing something to a rough-looking character on the dock. It's faint, but the shape is familiar, a bottle, perhaps....

The stamp would depict boat day. For the dozens of communities served by Union ships in the 1920s, boat day was the central event in their weekly calendar. It was when new valves for the broken steam donkey arrived, and yeast for the bread, and Carnation milk, and thread and grease and boom chains, saw files, yards of cloth, and cake from Woodwards, tweezers and salt and butter and serge pants and news.

Especially news. It's difficult to comprehend today how remote these areas were. No television, no newspapers. Maybe an old crystal radio squawked a bit of gossip. Mainly, though, the only society, day after day, was the dozen or two residents clustered in the little clapboard houses on the narrow beach above high tide.

Boat day became a part of coastal life soon after the *Comox* made its first run, in 1892. At that time settlers were so thankful for a regular link to civilization they uncritically considered the Union boats a miracle of sorts, their arrival worth recording for posterity in their journals, as Edith Bendickson observed was the case with her father, Port Neville pioneer Hans Hansen:

April 15, 1898: The Coquitlam *went aground on Frolander Reef and tore her keel off and put a hole in her. The steering gear went out of order.*

Feb. 16, 1899: Coquitlam *came at noon. One of the deckhands fell down the hatch and broke his ribs.*

October 19, 1904: Cassiar *came at 8 o'clock in the morning. Tried to put the cattle (Molly and Johnny) on board but could not get them on, as they had no proper gangplanks with them. Cattle fell in the bay and swam home.*

By 1920, however, the attitude toward the Union had undergone a change. No longer was the service considered a privilege; the Union company was now one of the family, and as such subject to all the criticism reserved for next of kin. Some took to calling them Union Stink Ships. This was partly a reference to the belch of foul smoke the ships inevitably released while docking, and partly a reference to the fact that in the minds of many, the company's service stunk. For residents from Rivers Inlet south, it seemed Union

Above: The *Lady Evelyn* shows why many passengers found the excessive smoke irritating and which resulted in the "stink ship" label.

Left: The *Lady Cecilia* in Pender Harbour. Union steamers loomed, literally and figuratively, in the lives of coastal settlements.

A.B.C. Sailing Guide

	Northbound Leave Vancouver (Union Pier)	Southbound Leave
Alert Bay Cannery	Tues. 8.00 p.m.	Sun. 9.00 a.m.
	Fri. 9.00 p.m.	Thur.
Alert Bay (Cook's Wharf)①	Tues. 8.00 p.m.	
Alice Arm	Fri. 9.00 a.m.	Wed. a.m.⑦
Anvil Island (Boat Landing)	Wed. 9.00 a.m.	Wed. a.m.⑦
(Southbound)	Fri. 9.00 a.m.	Fri. p.m.
Anyox	Fri. 9.00 p.m.	Mon. 10.15 a.m.⑦
Arrandale④ (Fortnightly)	Fri. 9.00 p.m.	Mon. p.m.⑦
B. & K. Logging Co.	Mon. 6.00 p.m.	Wed. a.m.
	Thur. 6.00 p.m.	Fri. a.m.⑦
Beaver Cove① (Fortnightly)	Tues. 8.00 p.m.	Sun. a.m.
Beaver Creek⑥ (Monthly)	Mon. 6.00 p.m.	Tues. p.m.⑦
Bella Bella	Tues. 8.00 p.m.	
Bella Bella Cannery	Tues. 8.00 p.m.	Sat. p.m.
Bella Coola	Tues. 8.00 p.m.	Thur. a.m.
Bishop Bay ① (Fortnightly)	Tues. 8.00 p.m.	Fri. a.m.⑤
Blind Channel Cannery	Mon. 6.00 p.m.	Tues. a.m.⑦
Bliss Landing	Tues. 9.30 a.m.	Sun. a.m.
Bloedel	Mon. 6.00 p.m.	Wed. 6.00 a.m.
	Thur. 6.00 p.m.	Sun. 7.00 a.m.
Blubber Bay	Tues. 9.30 a.m.	Wed. a.m.
	Thur. 9.30 a.m.	Fri. p.m.
	Sat. 2.00 p.m.	Sun. a.m.
Bold Point	Tues. 9.30 a.m.	Wed. a.m.
Bones Bay ⑤ (By request)	Thur. 6.00 p.m.	Fri. p.m.⑦
Bowen Island	Weekdays (Ex. Tues.) 9.00 a.m.	⎱ Weekdays (ex. Tues.) 5.00 p.m.
	Also Sat. 2.00 p.m.	⎰ Sun. 8.15 a.m.
Britannia Beach	Weekdays (Ex. Tues.) 9.00 a.m.	Weekdays (ex. Tues.) 3.00 p.m.
Broughton Logging Co.	Thur. 6.00 p.m.	Sat. a.m.⑦
Buccaneer Bay	Tues. 9.30 a.m.	Wed. and
	⑤Sat. 2.00 p.m.	Sun. p.m.*
Butedale	Tues. 8.00 p.m.	Tues. p.m.
	Fri. 9.00 p.m.	Sat. a.m.
Bute Inlet (Via Stuart Island only)		
Campbell River	Mon. 6.00 p.m.	Wed. 8.00 a.m.
	Tues. 8.00 p.m.	Sun. 9.00 a.m.
	Thur. 6.00 p.m.	
Cartwright Bay	Thur. 6.00 p.m.	Sat. p.m.⑦
Channel Logging Co.	Thur. 6.00 p.m.	Sat. a.m.⑦
Charles Creek	Thur. 6.00 p.m.	Sat. a.m.⑦
Chonat Bay	Thur. 6.00 p.m.	Fri. a.m.⑦
Churchouse	Thur. 9.30 a.m.	Fri. a.m.
Claxton Cannery	Tues. 8.00 p.m.	Fri. p.m.⑦
Cowan's Point	⑤ Tues. 9.00 a.m.	Tues. p.m.
	Sat. 9.00 a.m.	Sun. p.m.
Dawson's Landing	Tues. 8.00 p.m.	Thur. a.m.⑦
Dempsey's Camp	Thur. 6.00 p.m.	Sat. a.m.⑦
Devaney's Camp	Thur. 6.00 p.m.	Sat. a.m.⑦
D. & F. Camp③	Fri. 9.00 a.m.	Fri. p.m.⑦
Earle & Brown	Thur. 6.00 p.m.	Sat. a.m.⑦
Eastbourne⑤	Mon. and Tues. 9.00 a.m.	
Echo Bay	Thur. 6.00 p.m.	Sat. a.m.⑦
Elk Bay	Mon. 6.00 p.m.	Wed. a.m.
	Thur. 6.00 p.m.	Sun. a.m.
Elkin's Point	Thur. 9.00 a.m.	Thur. p.m.⑦
Englewood	Tues. 8.00 p.m.	Sun. a.m.
	Fri. 9.00 p.m.	Thurs. a.m.
Eng's Camp	Mon. 6.00 p.m.	Tues. p.m.⑦
Frederick Arm	Mon. 6.00 p.m.	Tues. p.m.⑦
False Bay (Lasqueti)	Mon. 6.00 p.m.	Wed. 11.30 a.m.
Garden Bay	Tues. 9.30 a.m.	*Wed., Fri. p.m.
	Thur. 9.30 a.m.	*Sun. p.m.
Garrett (Menzies Bay)	Mon. 6.00 p.m.	Wed. a.m.
	Thur. 6.00 p.m.	Sun. a.m.
Gibson's Landing	Mon., Tues., Wed., Fri. and Sat. 9.00 a.m.	⎱ Weekdays (ex. Thur.) p.m.
	Sat. 2.00 p.m.	⎰ Sun. 6.45 p.m.
Gower Point⑤	Tues. 9.30 a.m.	*Wed., Fri.
	Sat. 2.00 p.m.	& Sun. p.m.
Grace Harbour	Fri. 9.00 a.m.	⎱ Fri. and
	Sat. 2.00 p.m.	⎰ Sun. p.m.
Granite Bay	Mon. 6.00 p.m.	Tues. a.m.⑦
Granite Island	Tues. 9.30 a.m.	Wed. a.m.

①Call made fortnightly on sailings from Vancouver of November 14, 28; December 12, 26; January 9, 23; February 6, 20; March 6, 20.
③Call will be made by request only.
④Call will be made fortnightly from Vancouver on sailings of November 3, 17; December 1, 15, 29; January 26; February 9, 23; March 9, 23.
⑥Call made monthly on sailings of November 20, December 18, January 15, February 12, March 12.
†All passengers and freight for Bute Inlet points will be handled to Stuart Island only. *Flag.

		Northbound Leave Vancouver (Union Pier)	Southbound Leave
Grantham's Lndg.	Mon., Tues., Wed., Fri. and Sat.	9.00 a.m.	⎱ Daily (ex.
	Sat.	2.00 p.m.	⎰ Thur.) p.m.
Grassey Bay		Mon. 6.00 p.m.	Tues. p.m.
Half Moon Bay	Tues. and Thur.	9.30 a.m.	⎱ Wed., Fri.
	Sat.	2.00 p.m.	⎰ and Sun. p.m.
Hardy Island		Tues. 9.30 a.m.	Fri. p.m.
Hartley Bay	③(Monthly)	Tues. 8.00 p.m.	Fri. a.m.⑦
Hayden Bay		Mon. 6.00 p.m.	Tues. p.m.⑦
Heriot Bay		Tues. 9.30 a.m.	Wed. a.m.⑦
Hillside	Tues. and Thur.	9.00 a.m.	Tues., Thur.
	Sat.	2.00 p.m.	and Sun. p.m.
Hopkins' Landing	Mon., Tues., Wed., Fri. and Sat.	9.00 a.m.	⎱ Daily (ex.
	Sat.	2.00 p.m.	⎰ Thur.) p.m.
Hyder, Alaska (Via Stewart, B.C.)			
Jackson Bay		Mon. 6.00 p.m.	Tues. p.m.⑦
Jamieson's Camp		Thur. 6.00 p.m.	Sat. a.m.⑦
Keats Island⑤	Mon., Wed. and Sat.	9.00 a.m.	Sun.⑤ p.m.
	Sat.	2.00 p.m.	
Kincolith		Fri. 9.00 p.m.	Mon. p.m.⑦
Kingcome Inlet		Thur. 6.00 p.m.	Sat. a.m.⑦
Kitamat (Once Monthly by arrangement)			
Klemtu (Fortnightly) (S'thbound)①		Tues. 8.00 p.m.	Sat. p.m.
Kwatna②		Tues. 8.00 p.m.	Thur. a.m.⑦
Kwatsi Bay		Thur. 6.00 p.m.	Sat. a.m.⑦
La Farr & Dumaresq		Thur. 6.00 p.m.	Sat. a.m.⑦
Lamb Lumber Co.		Mon. 6.00 p.m.	Wed. 6.30 a.m.
		Thur. 6.00 p.m.	Sun. a.m.
Lang Bay		Tues. 9.30 a.m.	Wed. p.m.
		Sat. 2.00 p.m.	⎱ Fri. and Sun. p.m.
Long Bay		Fri. 9.00 a.m.	Fri. p.m.⑦
Longview	Tues. and Thur.	9.00 a.m.	Tues.,Thur.
	Sat.	2.00 p.m.	and Sun. p.m.
Loughboro Inlet		Mon. 6.00 p.m.	Tues. p.m.⑦
Lowe Inlet①	(Monthly)	Tues. 8.00 p.m.	
Lund	Tuesday and Thur.	9.30 a.m.	Wed. a.m.
	(Southbound only) Sat.	2.00 p.m.	⎱ Fri. and Sun. a.m.
McLellan Logging Co.		Thur. 6.00 p.m.	Sat. a.m.⑦
McNab Creek	Tues. and Thur.	9.00 a.m.	Tues., Thur.
	Sat.	2.00 p.m.	and Sun. a.m.
Madeira Park	⑤	Tues. 9.30 a.m.	
Manson's Landing		Tues. 9.30 a.m.	Wed. a.m.
	(Southbound only) Thur.	9.30 a.m.	⎱ Fri. and Sun. a.m.
Margaret Bay④	(Monthly)	Tues. 8.00 p.m.	Wed. p.m.⑦
Menzies Bay		Mon. 6.00 p.m.	Wed. a.m.
		Thur. 6.00 p.m.	Sun. a.m.
Merry Island		Tues. 9.30 a.m.	*Wed. and
		Sat. 2.00 p.m.	Fri. p.m.
Minstrel Island		Thur. 6.00 p.m.	Sun. a.m.
Namu		Tues. 8.00 p.m.	Wed. p.m.
		Fri. 9.00 p.m.	Sat. p.m.
Nelson Island		Tues. 9.30 a.m.	Wed. p.m.
New Brighton	Tues., Thur. and Fri.	9.00 a.m.	⎱ Tues., Thur.
	Sat.	2.00 p.m.	⎰ Fri. and Sun. p.m.
Nodales		Mon. 6.00 p.m.	Tues. p.m.
O'Brien Bay		Thur. 6.00 p.m.	Sat. a.m.⑦
O'Brien (D. J.) Camp		Thur. 6.00 p.m.	Sat. a.m.⑦
Ocean Falls		Tues. 8.00 p.m.	Wed. 9.00 a.m.
Paisley Island⑤		Tues. 9.00 a.m.	
Parker & Palmer		Thur. 6.00 p.m.	Fri. a.m.⑦
Pender Harbour		Tues. 9.30 a.m.	⎱ Wed. p.m.
		Thur. 9.30 a.m.	⎰ Fri. p.m.
(Irvine's Landing only)	Sat.	2.00 p.m.	⎰ Sun. p.m.
Plowden Bay		Thur. 9.00 a.m.	Thur. p.m.⑦
			Sun. p.m.
Porcher Is. Cannery⑤	(By req.)	Tues. 8.00 p.m.	Fri. p.m.⑦
Port Elizabeth		Thur. 6.00 p.m.	Fri. a.m.⑦
Port Hardy (Hardy Bay)		Tues. 8.00 p.m.	Sun. 6.00 a.m.
		Fri. 9.00 p.m.	Wed. p.m.
Port Harvey (Cracroft)		Thur. 6.00 p.m.	Sun. a.m.
Port Mellon	Tues. and Thur.	9.00 a.m.	Tues. p.m.⑦
	Sat.	2.00 p.m.	Sun. p.m.
Port Neville		Thur. 6.00 p.m.	Sun. a.m.
Port Simpson		Fri. 9.00 p.m.	Mon. a.m.⑦

①Call made fortnightly on sailings from Vancouver of November 14, 28; December 12, 26; January 9, 23; February 6, 20; March 6, 20.
②Call made fortnightly on sailings from Vancouver of November 7, 21; December 5, 19; January 2, 16, 30; February 13, 27; March 13, 27.
③Call made monthly on sailings from Vancouver of November 7, December 5, January 2, February 6, March 6.
④Call made monthly on sailings from Vancouver of November 28, December 26, January 23, February 20, March 20.
⑤Call will be made by request only.
⑦Call made on northbound trip only. *Flag.

	Northbound Leave Van (Union P
Porteau (Boat Landing)	⑤Fri. 9.0
Powell River (See Page 4)	Fri. 9.0
Prince Rupert	Tues. 8.0
Provincial Cannery③ (Fortnightly)	Tues. 8.0
Quathiaski Cove	Mon. 6.0
	Thur. 6.0
Ramsay Arm	Thur. 6.0
	Sat. 2.0
Read Island	Thur. 9.3
Redonda Bay	Thur. 9.3
	Sat. 2.0
Refuge Cove	Sat. 2.0
Rivers Inlet Cannery③	Tues. 8.0
Roberts' Creek	Tues. and Thur. 9.0
	Sat. 2.0
Rock Bay	Mon. 6.0
	Thur. 6.0
Roy	Mon. 6.0
Rotus Camp	Thur. 6.0
Savary Island	Tues. 9.3
	⑤Thur. 9.3
	Sat. 2.0
Sayward	Mon. 6.0
Scott Cove Logging Co.	Thur. 6.0
Seaford	Thur. 6.0
Seaside Park	Tues. and Thur. 9.0
	Sat. 2.0
Sechelt	Sun. 9.0
	Thur. 9.0
	Sat. 2.0
Selma Park	Tues. 9.0
	⑤Sat. 2.0
Shoal Bay	Mon. 6.0
Shushartie Bay	Tues. 8.0
Simoon Sound	Thur. 6.0
Skeena River Canneries (See Page 2)	Tues. 8.0
Soderman's Camp	Tues. 8.0
Sointula	Tues. 8.0
	Fri. 9.0
Squamish	Weekdays (except Tues.) 9.
Squirrel Cove	Thur. 9.
Stag Bay (Southbound)	Thur. 9.
Stewart	Fri. 9.
Stillwater	Tues. 9.
	Thur. 9.
	Sat. 2.
Stuart Island	Thur. 6.
Surge Narrows	Tues. 9.
Sullivan Bay	Thur. 6.
Swanson Bay	Tues. 8.
Takahashi Camp	Thur. 6.
Tallheo Cannery ①(Fortnightly)	Tues. 8.
Telegraph Cove ①(Fortnightly)	Tues. 8.
Turner Island Logging Co.	Thur. 6.
Van Anda	Tues. 9.
	Thur. 9.
	Sat. 2.
Vaucroft Beach	Tues. 9.
Wadham's Cannery	Tues. 8.
Wahkina Bay	Thur. 6.
Wakeman Sound	Thur. 6.
Wales Island (See Special Note)⑤	Fri. 9.
West Bay	Fri. 9
Westview (Powell River)	Tues. and Thur. 9.
	Sat. 2.
Whaletown	Tues. 9.
(Southbound only)	Thur. 9
Willett's Camp	Thur. 9
Wilson Creek	Tues. 9.
	Sat. 2
Woodfibre	Weekdays (except Tues.) 9
Y.M.C.A. Camp⑤	Thurs. and Fri. 9

①Call made fortnightly on sailings from Vancou... December 12, 26; January 9, 23; February 6...
②Call made fortnightly on sailings from Vancou... ber 5, 19; January 2, 16, 30; February 13, 27...
⑤Call will be made by arrangement only.
⑦Call made on northbound trip only. *Flag.

schedules were only predictable in that they were unpredictable. Al Lloyd, former store manager at Pender Harbour, recalled the problem: "To get out of the Harbour there was the Union Steamship boat sailing south, three times a week, or a fish boat. The choice was more or less yours. The Union boat would phone Bill Matier at Irvine's Landing with an ETA, which was at best an approximation and at worst a downright lie. The boat mostly got here when it got here. Waiting for hours on the wharf on a hot summer day could and did get pretty tedious. I remember a time when I took a guest over to catch the boat at noon, having previously checked that it was expected about 12:30. We waited for a long while, roasting in the sun. Finally I took our guest home for a swim, and then back again to the wharf, another long wait and I took her home for supper, back to the wharf again and the boat finally arrived at 8:30 p.m. Never did have the heart to enquire when it got to town.

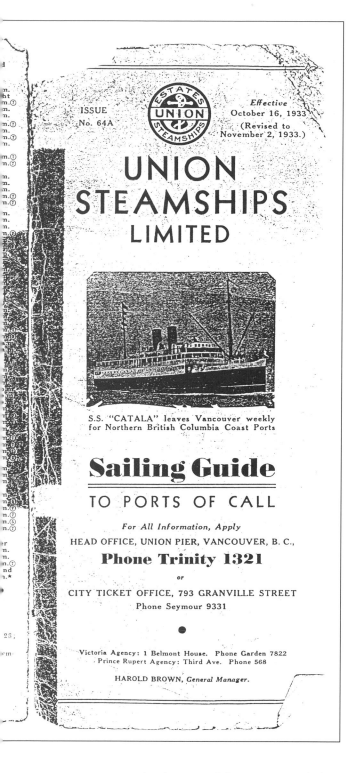

**Above: An eclectic crowd awaits the Union steamer at Gower
Point, on the Sunshine Coast.**

Left: Union vessels sailed more than 5000 miles a week.

"Anyhow the trip could take anywhere from five to ten hours, and it was a brave person who asked friends to meet them at the boat, or made an appointment for the same day."

One of the enduring discussions about the Union ships was how they could possibly be so late. They seemed to trundle in at any time, with no relation to bad weather, tides or time of year. People wondered aloud about the unscheduled jaunts Union crews must be taking. Victoria? Seattle? Honolulu? By comparison, CPR vessels seemed to be able to stick to schedules. Why couldn't Union ships, they demanded, do the same?

The answer, of course, is that the two companies were not working the same type of routes. For the most part, CPR ships served main ports, with proper unloading and dock facilities. Union ships, on the other hand, served many more little stops, often unloading at rickety floats, or even into rowboats in open water. And they lugged a more eclectic cargo. More stops, varied cargo: the inevitable result was unexpected delays that put ships behind schedule. (It's significant that North Coast residents, served by Union ships making fewer stops than those on the busy south coast routes, claimed they could set their clocks by the arrival of a Union ship.)

Another argument that grew out of the Union service to small communities had to do with settlement of the coast. In 1890, when the Union company was just starting, there were probably fewer than one thousand settlers between Howe Sound and Prince Rupert. During the 1920s, when the Union company was at its peak, there were as many as twenty thousand people in the same area. Was the population increase a cause—or consequence—of the Union service?

As early as 1894, the *Vancouver Daily News-Advertiser* was offering an answer: "Many people are probably not aware that a large number of settlers are located along the coast of the Mainland, and on the numerous islands between here and Port Neville. Though somewhat slow, the increase in settlement has gone on surely, until now there must be some hundreds of people living on different ranches in this locality. The establishment of weekly steamship service between this city and these settlements by the Union Steamship Co. of British Columbia has in large measure induced many to locate on these islands, and to the Union Steamship Co. a large amount of credit is due."

By the 1920s it had become a fact of life on the coast that if a community or camp was to survive, it had to have Union service. Not only did Union ships bring supplies, but they brought information and fresh blood from the outside that kept communities from stagnating and camps from closing down. For example, Union steamer service was so important that Merrill, Ring & Moore's camp in Theodosia Inlet actually guaranteed the company a certain number of passengers every time the company vessel pulled in. The way they did this was by having the camp superintendent fire the required number of loggers on ship day. No matter that the men might be good at their jobs—the quota had to be met. It was said the camp had three crews: one in the woods, one in town, one on the ship.

For coastal residents fortunate enough to have radios, the first news that the Union steamer's arrival was imminent was the schedule broadcast. As a Union ship worked its way along a route, the captain would often radio ahead to the next stop. Coastal resident Edith Bendickson once recalled the cheerful voice of Captain Wilson saying, "Hello, hello,

hello! This is the steamer *Venture* calling with approximate arrival times!" Sometimes, when a passenger was on board, Captain Wilson would add their name to the "sked" broadcast. "Mrs. Hansen is on board for Port Neville!"

For those without radios, the only way to make sure they didn't miss the Union boat was simply by going to the dock and waiting. They gathered on the dock, rolled cigarettes out of the dregs of a can of MacDonald's tobacco, swapped stories, spat on the tide and, all the time, kept one ear cocked for that long, piercing series of whistles that told them the Union boat was just around the point. The Union company whistle was the Morse code "X"—one long, two short, one long—and it echoed up the long and narrow inlets for miles. To a well-trained ear, though, the whistle on each Union ship had a distinctive sound. Savary Island pioneer Jim Spilsbury claimed he could tell when the *Cowichan* was heading in because its whistle started low and graduated to a steady pitch, the result of hot steam condensing on the cold metal of the whistle.

For Union crews the sound of the whistle meant it was time to go to work. With ships often scheduled to make several dozen stops in a day, crews had to work quickly to get the ship docked, unload supplies, mail and passengers, then check in anyone boarding and cast off for the next point on the route. To company officials in Vancouver, with their charts of schedules, it seemed as if this should be a mechanical procedure. Ship in, unload, ship out. In reality, there were a thousand things that could foul up a docking.

The most serious was fog. The echo of a ship's whistle was a reliable measure for staying away from rocks, but it became less accurate the closer a vessel got to

Above: The *Cowichan* offloading at a gyppo logger's raft.

Left: Residents of communities too small to afford a proper dock, or in an area where a dock was too difficult to built, arrived on and departed from steamers via large floats.

Once Union navigators had a ship docked they often took time to chat with locals.

land. What navigators needed was noise from the shore to guide them in. This is where the empty forty-five-gallon drum played a role in BC's history. An empty drum hammered with sticks guided many Union vessels safely alongside a fog-shrouded dock. Barking dogs were also helpful, as was a flat shovel pounded vigorously with a hammer. At least one coastal resident guided a ship in by playing "Westering Home" on the bagpipes.

But even in clear weather docking could be a troublesome procedure. Each cove had its own patterns of wind and current that had to be understood. Take Salmon River, in Kelsey Bay. Union ships always made a starboard landing at Salmon River on account of the currents. One time a new navigator was bringing the *Capilano* into Salmon River. The *Capilano*'s captain at the time, John Park, told him about the current. The newcomer said, "I can manage a port landing all right." He promptly crashed the vessel into the dock, shaking every timber. There was a brief gasp among the crew, as there were twenty-one tons of dynamite in the *Capilano*'s bow.

Then there were the idiosyncrasies of each navigator. Every captain and chief officer, it seemed, had his own ideas about the definitive way to dock a ship. One liked to take his ship in head first, then jimmy it around. Another brought his vessel in alongside the dock, then warped it in with a springline. Chief officer Jack Summerfield, also known as "Anxious Moments," would mutter to himself, "She'll never make it, she'll never make it." Capt. Bob Wilson liked to sit on the bridge rail, legs over the forward side, and operate the telegraph with his hands behind his back, as if he were a basketball hotshot.

Some captains never did get the hang of docking. Capt. Howard Lawrey, for example. Born at sea, he had spent most of his life aboard ships before joining the Union company in 1917. He was one of the company's best navigators, yet he always had trouble

Capt. Howard Lawrey relaxing at Savary Island. He was with the Union company from 1917–1945.

docking. Once, while pulling into Roberts Creek (north of Langdale) on a northbound run, Lawrey's ship sliced off the front of the local wharf. On the southbound call at the same port he took out some more piles. The wharfinger was livid. It was springtime and his wharf would be out of service all season. "What the hell did you bother coming back for?" he hollered up to Lawrey, who was on the bridge. Lawrey snapped back, "Just to cover up the damage we did on the way up."

Docking wasn't made any easier if a captain had been boozing. A navigator might get away with drinking while the ship was en route, but when it came to the delicate job of bringing a 1300-ton steamer alongside a rickety, half-sunk wharf in a small inlet, the effects of liquor showed. Capt. Robert Naughty was one of these navigators. He was infamous for his drinking, and his clunky landings. (Captain Naughty is on record as having made only one really good docking in his entire Union career. This was when approaching the Union dock in Vancouver one evening. He brought his vessel alongside the wharf so smoothly and gracefully, they could've been waltzing partners. Unfortunately, in his intoxicated state, he'd mistaken the Evans, Coleman, Evans dock for the Union dock. They were about one hundred yards apart. Captain Naughty realized his mistake when nobody rushed over to take his lines. He quickly reversed to the Union dock, but it was too late. His error was noticed and the next day he was relieved of his command.)

Even when conditions were ideal and the navigator was sober, it seemed there were any number of things that could go wrong while docking. One time the Union's SS *Chilco* was easing into a wharf in an otherwise perfect landing when an anchor davit became lodged under some timbers. The ship was still moving forward, and the davit dug

Above left:
Capt. Bob Naughty

Above right:
Chief officer Jack Summerfield

Even a modest-sized steamer like the *Chilco* (151 feet long, 22 feet wide) could do a lot of damage to a wharf. In 1935 the *Chilco* was renamed *Lady Pam.*

Arrival of the *Lady Alexandra*, which could carry two thousand passengers, made for busy days at small settlements like Selma Park.

into the wharf like a hook into a salmon's mouth. There it was, snagged under the wharf and unable to back out. Fortunately, the mate at the time knew there were fallers aboard going back up-coast to their logging camp. Fallers always carried their saws, axes, wedges and other tools so he asked them if they would like to cut the boat free. Fallers usually practise their art deep in the woods, far from view, and this pair evidently enjoyed the idea of performing for a crowd. While crew and passengers watched, they sawed through the bull rail and the heavy planks and the *Chilco* was able to ease away.

Deckhands had an important role in docking as well. When a ship got close to a wharf, the captain would holler, "Throw the lines." Then a deckhand would heave a heavy coil of rope to the wharf, where it would be secured. When a captain worked a ship in close to a dock, this was an easy task. The concept of "close" was an ambiguous one. For lousy ship-dockers, "close" meant wherever the ship happened to be when they ran out of patience. Thus, the deckhand's job was not for greenhorns. One time a Union navigator

Chelohsin at Quathiaski Cove.

notorious for his bad dockings, Paddy Hannigan, was bringing the *Chelohsin* into Quathiaski Cove, off Discovery Passage, just north of Campbell River. Quathiaski was a difficult place to dock for the best of navigators because Grouse Island takes up so much of the cove and the currents are very strong. Hannigan was having a terrible time, jimmying the ship back and forth, when he gave up in exasperation. "Throw the line!" he screamed to the deckhand on the bow. The distance from the *Chelohsin* to the dock was such that it would have taxed the most seasoned sailor. But the deckhand, a young man named Hinnigan, was new on the job. He coiled the line and, responding to the thrill of the moment, flung the rope and himself overboard. This only exacerbated Hannigan's fury, and the ship was launched into chaos. Hinnigan was rescued eventually, and the *Chelohsin* had to try docking once again.

The captain's work ended once the steamer was docked. Celebrities of sorts, captains would often idle around the decks, trading stories and gossip with people gathered on the dock below. Meanwhile, the pursers and deck crews had to try to get the mail and cargo off as fast as possible. A gangplank was run out, and winches whined as pallets (or boards, as they were called) of cargo were swung from below decks onto the dock. It was a hectic, noisy time, with orders hollered back and forth.

A calm day at Campbell River. The dock is in approximately the same location as the current government wharf.

This job was especially difficult if the water was rough. Campbell River was often a particularly turbulent place. Before the breakwater was built, waves pounded the little dock regularly. Aboard the Union ship, it seemed as if you were on a seesaw. One minute the dock was far above the ship's deck; the next minute the ship was towering above the dock. The gangplank bucked like a mule. Passengers were helped ashore with extra ropes and crew members carried the children. Occasionally, the weather was so bad that only passengers could be unloaded—the cargo had to stay aboard. And if things got too rough, then the ship carried on and passengers and cargo got a free tour of the coast.

Besides rough water, there were two things that made dockside work difficult for deckhands. One of these was heavy equipment. An inevitable part of serving logging camps was muscling tons of equipment off a ship's deck and onto a rickety dock. Sometimes this was accomplished with brute muscle; other times it required ingenuity. A Port Neville resident recalled one occasion and the troubles the *Cassiar* crew had in getting a bull gear for a steam donkey up a steep wharf. Ropes were applied, and all hands available pushed and heaved—all to no avail. Finally an enterprising individual took a slab of side bacon and greased the dock. The rigging was then reapplied and—up the wharf went the gear. (What happened to anyone stepping on the dock afterwards was not mentioned.)

The other problem cargo was animals. Union ships carried every type of barnyard animal, including cattle. Cattle had a nasty trick of dashing in one cargo door and right out the other, into the drink. Then deckhands would be assigned to rowboats to herd

Posing for photos was part of an officer's duties.

Animals were never an easy cargo. This horse attempted to swim ashore after jumping out the cargo doors of the *Lady Alexandra*, Vancouver, about 1936.

the wayward livestock ashore and onto the dock, where they would try loading them again.

No matter how long a ship remained dockside, the departure was always a frenzied affair. Winches had to be secured, cargo lashed, and new passengers assigned rooms. Inevitably, someone arrived at the last minute with a package. One up-coast resident, forester Ron Jones, recalled arriving so late he had to hurl a package aboard a Union vessel as it was pulling away from the dock. The package was for his wife in Vancouver. A deckhand on the bow caught the bundle and, in the hurly burly of leaving, passed it to another deckhand. He passed the package to yet another deckhand and so it went down the deck from hand to hand. Finally it ended up in the arms of a puzzled crew member on the stern, who took a hasty glance at the parcel, saw a scrawled name, and called to Jones on the dock, "Here, this is for you," heaving the package back to him.

During the 1920s, when Union steamers were calling at over 150 ports and settlements, it was said that nothing was too small for a company to deliver. Union crews would, if asked, take a single letter into a remote camp. That opinion, while not incorrect, wasn't quite the case. There were places Union ships wouldn't dock—either because a bay or cove was too difficult to get into, or because there wasn't enough business to warrant a position on a regular route. This often happened with small gyppo loggers, whose operations literally dotted the coast. But the company didn't abandon these customers. Instead, it developed several methods for getting cargo from the Union ship to these operations without the ship having to leave the safe waters of a main passageway.

One of these methods was simply throwing a package or parcel overboard at a prearranged point. Gyppo loggers often got parts this way. They would send or radio notice down to a Vancouver supplier that they needed a certain piece of equipment "packed to float." The supplier would take the part, slather it in grease, then seal it in an empty kerosene can marked with a flag. Union crews would take the can, and at the proper moment pitch it overboard. Ideally, the logger would be waiting in a smaller boat and quickly scoop up the bucket. Otherwise, he came out later and found the bucket bobbing approximately where it had been left.

The other method for transferring cargo entailed passing it directly from the Union ship into a waiting boat. This was a common but specialized procedure that required synchronization between both vessels. The way it usually worked was a Union ship would pull up off a settlement and turn so the cargo doors were to the lee of the prevailing wind. Then little boats would move alongside and cargo would be passed down. It was a wobbly, unsteady procedure, and more than one case of canned milk ended up on the bottom of a strait. And if the transfer was made without a hitch, there was always the problem of the little craft breaking the "pull" of the bigger craft. Longtime coast residents learned to head for the bow of the bigger ship, then suddenly cut away, where they were free to row back with their cargo.

Such a tricky manoeuvre inevitably resulted in disasters. A Union ship was delivering cargo to a Scottish farmer who lived near Powell River, on a lonely stretch of land between Lang Bay and Stillwater. This farmer, as he had done many times before, rowed out to the Union ship to fetch his mail and a few supplies, which included two bales of hay. The mail was transferred, as was the hay. Then the farmer reminded the crew there was something else. "Ha ye got some horseshoes for me," he hollered. There was a scramble, and a deckhand produced a large bundle of horseshoes, thoughtfully wired together. Then he tossed the bundle overboard. The horseshoes hit the bottom of the farmer's little boat and vanished. A moment later, a geyser appeared between the farmer's legs. Worried more about his precious hay than his own life, he set off—rowing madly—for shore.

A Union steamer as seen by the many settlers and gyppo loggers who rowed out for supplies. Cargo was transferred through an open cargo door.

Chapter Six

1925-1929:
Cardena and Catala

*Masters and Officers must distinctly understand that the safe navigation of the ship is to be, in all instances,
their first consideration. They must run no risk, which, by any possibility, might result in accident.
They must always bear in mind that the safety of life and property entrusted to their care is the ruling principle by
which they must be governed in the navigation of their ship, and no saving of time on their voyage is to be sought
at the risk of accident.*

Item 18, Standing Orders of the Union Steamship Company of British Columbia, Limited

S everal years after World War One, it became obvious to Union
company officials and crews that ships of the current fleet were
incapable of meeting the demands of the booming coastal economy.
This was especially true of vessels on the northern runs—to Prince
Rupert and the canneries of the Nass and Skeena Rivers—where the stalwart *Camosun* and
Venture were kept in virtual nonstop service. A single crack-up and the company would lose
customers to the aggressive Canadian Pacific or Canadian National steamer fleets.

With this less than ideal situation in mind, in late 1922 the company let out
a contract to Napier & Miller, of Old Kilpatrick, Scotland, for construction of a new ship.
This vessel was to be based on the SS *Venture*. Built in 1910 and acquired by the Union
company with the purchase of the Boscowitz line in 1911, the *Venture* proved an excellent
craft, capable of dealing with the heavy seas often encountered in crossing Queen Charlotte
Sound. Large cargo hatches also made it ideal for the cannery run, where quick turnarounds
in loading were imperative if a vessel wasn't to get trapped inshore by a low tide. The ship's
only drawback was lack of refrigeration, which meant meats had to be stored on deck. It was
said that in summer you could smell the *Venture* coming before you could hear its whistle.

Using the *Venture*'s basic hull design, engineers at Napier & Miller added
fifty feet to the length and slightly over five feet to the beam. They also added a refrigeration
compartment capable of holding thirty tons of frozen fish. The new vessel was to have a
steerage section for cannery workers, forty-two cabins with hot and cold water (that, in itself,

**Opposite:
Flagship of the Union
fleet during the 1920s
and '30s, the *Cardena*
is pictured here at
Stuart Island. Thurlow
Island is in the
background.**

The seaworthy *Venture* was built for the Victoria-based Boscowitz Steamship Co. in 1910, and named after an earlier *Venture* which had burned at Inverness Cannery.

was enough to make it a flagship), two suites with private baths, a large observation room, a sixty-eight-seat dining room, and a two-hatch cargo hold capable of carrying 350 tons of freight.

The result, launched on the Clyde on March 22, 1923, was the SS *Cardena*, the biggest ship to operate under the Union flag to date. Slightly over 226 feet long, it was more than twice the size of the original *Comox*. It was also the first Union vessel to depart from the tradition of Indian place names beginning with "C": Cardena Bay, on Kennedy Island at the mouth of the Skeena River, was named after Captain Cardenas, an early Spanish explorer.

Capt. Andy Johnstone

The *Cardena* steamed into Vancouver on June 11, 1923. Nine days later it sailed right back out, bound for Prince Rupert. The layover was unusually brief because company officials were eager to hear how the new vessel performed. It was twelve years since the Union had taken delivery of a new, steel-hulled, combination passenger/freighter. The last was the *Chelohsin*, in 1911. Would the *Cardena* be a roaring success, like the *Chelohsin*? Or a disaster, like the second-to-last new vessel, the *Cheslakee*? (That name wasn't even mentioned around the Carrall Street dock.)

The answer wasn't long in coming. Within days, news from up-coast was that the *Cardena* was an excellent ship. In coming weeks the praise got even higher. The ship was, declared its officers and crew, the best of the fourteen ships the company was operating at the time, including the prototype *Venture*. They cited as evidence the way the *Cardena* handled rough water—easily, and with little of the side slipping that characterized less seaworthy ships. (And so the praise continued for years and years until, by the 1950s, many Union navigators comfortably claimed that the *Cardena* was the finest of the fifty-three vessels the company ever owned or operated.)

Several years after it went into service, the *Cardena* was placed under the command of Capt. Andy Johnstone. Known as the "Cannery Skipper," Johnstone was a dashing, squint-eyed figure, given to chewing out crews for anything less than perfection in their duties. (Appropriately, Johnstone shared Dumfrieshire, England, as a birthplace with the swashbuckling American admiral and pirate, John Paul Jones.) He had moved to BC when still young, and literally grew up around the Union docks at the turn of the century.

By the time he took over command of the *Cardena*, Captain Johnstone's reputation as a navigator was already established. This reputation was largely a result of his

actions aboard the *Venture* on September 16, 1922. The *Venture* was loading salmon at a Skeena River cannery early in the morning when it received an SOS on the wireless. The Seattle-based SS *Queen*, carrying a full load of passengers from Alaska, had gone aground on Whitecliff Island, twelve miles away on the east side of Chatham Sound. A breathless Sparks (all radio operators were called "Sparks") took the message to Captain Johnstone, who immediately ordered a reply sent to say the *Venture* was on its way.

There was a thick fog lying off the Skeena that day, and it took Captain Johnstone some time to make his way out of the Skeena's tangle of channels to open water. Then he spent almost two hours easing westward, probing the wall of white mist with the ship's whistle, waiting for an answer, by which to locate the *Queen*. When the *Venture* finally pulled alongside, the crew discovered the American ship high on a reef, with 238 passengers milling anxiously around the stern, eager to be off. Captain Johnstone manoeuvred the *Venture* so its bow was close enough to the *Queen*'s stern for a gangplank, and the army of passengers, complete with luggage, trundled across. It was a bold move, as it placed the *Venture* only feet from the rocks that holed the *Queen*. Then, when everyone was transferred,

During the 1920s the *Cardena* ran upcoast to Prince Rupert; the copper mine at Anyox, in Observatory Inlet; and the Dolly Varden silver mine in Alice Arm.

the *Venture* eased back through the fog to deposit everyone safely in Prince Rupert. Many of the *Queen*'s passengers were so impressed with Captain Johnstone that they booked passage south on the *Venture*—a fact the Union company was at pains to point out to press covering the event.

Whatever it was about Captain Johnstone that attracted adventure didn't dissipate when he took over the *Cardena*. On August 22, 1927, Johnstone and the *Cardena* were making their way south through Seymour Narrows in a patchy fog that limited visibility to one hundred yards. The narrows (just over 2000 feet wide) was a busy marine thoroughfare, and the *Cardena* was easing ahead, crew scanning the waters for sign of a bluff or another ship. Then the shrill of a ship's whistle penetrated the curtain of fog, followed by one, two, three, four more blasts. Five in all, the international code for ship in distress.

Again, Captain Johnstone didn't hesitate. He eased the *Cardena* toward the sound. What he found, looming out of the fog several minutes later, was the makings of a disaster. There, perched on treacherous Ripple Rock, sat the crack Canadian National liner *Prince Rupert*. It was badly grounded and listing, one of its propellers spinning futilely, like the autonomic twitchings of a dying sockeye.

It turned out the *Prince Rupert* had been on its way south, bucking an ebb tide, when it clipped the tip of Ripple Rock. The ship had passed clear, but been swept back by the powerful current. The second collision was far more severe than the first, and jammed

The Union's investors thought the company should have charged Canadian National for rescuing the *Prince Rupert* from Ripple Rock, but the firm's managers opted to cash in on the good publicity by waiving fees.

the ship's rudder into the starboard propeller. Stranded in one of the most tideswept channels on the coast, with a full load of passengers, the *Prince Rupert* was in a desperate situation.

Captain Johnstone eased the *Cardena* close to the *Prince Rupert*, and a heavy towing line was secured to the bow of the stranded ship. Then, in Johnstone's words, "working the *Cardena* in the manner of a tug moving a liner," they pulled the vessel off the rock. The operation went so well that Johnstone momentarily debated towing the *Prince Rupert* all the way to Vancouver. But the Rupert's jammed rudder made him think better of it. (Wisely, as it turned out. It took two powerful tugs to muscle the unstable *Rupert* back to Vancouver.) In the end, Johnstone settled for taking the *Prince Rupert* to nearby Deep Cove, where the passengers were off-loaded onto the *Cardena* and a passing Canadian Pacific ship, the *Princess Beatrice*. The event, widely reported at the time, was another coup for the Union company, who doubled the public's goodwill by declining any compensation for the rescue from Canadian National.

Even on uneventful runs Captain Johnstone transformed the *Cardena* into a much larger, more elegant ship than it actually was. He often cast himself as a social director, and would convene impromptu lessons on the intricacies of on-deck shuffleboard, or the finer points of knot-tying. He even encouraged crew members Tom and Ernie Lucas, Fred Tite and a fellow with the unlikely name of Johnnie Walker to form an on-board band. The Musical Mariners, as they were called, would set up in a lounge in the evening, and passengers danced as the *Cardena* made its way up the remote coast.

Captain Johnstone's tenure with the Union company was to last until 1932, when he went to the Pilotage. But before he left, he had a last grand adventure with the *Cardena*. This took place in the fall of 1931, in the narrow inlets around Ocean Falls. The *Cardena* and the CPR vessel *Princess Joan* were unloading freight one evening at Ocean Falls when they both received wireless messages from their respective organizations. A cannery at Bella Bella was overstocked with cases of canned salmon and was desperate for a ship or ships to relieve its inventory.

The *Cardena* loading salmon at Butedale in the 1930s.

The Union dock in late June 1924. Britain's largest warship,
the HMS *Hood* is departing from Vancouver through Burrard Inlet.

There was enough salmon at the cannery to load both the *Cardena* and the *Princess Joan*. The trouble for Captain Johnstone, however, was that if the *Princess Joan* got to Bella Bella first, it would occupy the only loading dock. The *Princess Joan* could load about five hundred cases an hour (compared to the *Cardena*'s fifteen hundred). At that rate the *Cardena* would have to wait for several hours, and consequently miss the tide on the Skeena River. And that, in turn, would throw the rest of the ship's schedule out of kilter.

Things got off to a bad start when the *Princess Joan* got away from the Ocean Falls docks fifteen minutes before the *Cardena*. It was faster than the *Cardena*, and was soon far down Fisher Channel. On the bridge, Captain Johnstone studied his options. The *Princess Joan*, he knew, was on its way to Lama Pass, the usual route to Bella Bella. But he also knew that about 10 km before Lama Pass there was an extremely small channel leading to Bella Bella called Gunboat Passage. Narrow and intricate, it was normally used by trollers and other small vessels to shortcut the distance between the two communities.

Minutes before reaching Gunboat Passage, Captain Johnstone ordered all the *Cardena*'s lights extinguished. He then quickly guided the ship into the narrows. For the next half hour the wheelhouse of the *Cardena* was a very intense place. Peering into the dusk, Johnstone frequently issued directions as the ship slid within yards of underwater rocks and reefs. Past Manson Point, past Anthony Point, past Nunn Point and its fringe of sunken boulders. Through the confines of Swept Channel. By Leila Island, Shave Point and the aptly named Flirt Island.

In the end, the gamble paid off. The *Cardena* made it to Bella Bella and had already loaded one thousand cases by the time the *Princess Joan* nosed into the harbour. Captain Johnstone couldn't resist a revengeful dig. "Don't worry," he hollered to the captain of the *Princess Joan*, "We'll be out of your way in another hour!"

Over the years, just about every major player in the Union company crossed the Cardena's decks. These included:

Billy McCombe Sr.

Billy McCombe Sr. A jowly, foul-mouthed Glaswegian, Capt. Billy McCombe worked the northern routes for years. Anything, he once said, was preferable to the tourist-laden southern runs. "On the passenger boats you had to get up every morning," he lamented. "You had to shave. You had to be forever dressed. You daren't go out to the wheelhouse rail to spit." To Billy McCombe fell the responsibility for dealing with the delivery of one of seven babies that were born on Union ships over the years. He recalled the event years later: *"We gave birth to a baby aboard ship. There was an experience for you, boy! Norm Pattison, the Chief steward, was there. If it hadn't been for Norm, I think that baby would have died. The freight clerks were sleeping down in the cabin ahead of this young fellow and his wife. She would be about nineteen, I think. He wasn't much older. When the pain started, she started to scream like bloody murder and the two freight clerks took off. They didn't know what the hell was happening. They just took off.*

"The chief steward come up to me and said, 'We've got a birth coming.' I said, 'Oh no, Christ no. Don't say that, Norman. She can't last out, eh?' 'No.' 'Oh, Jesus,' I said, 'we'd better get the book out.' We got the book out. You ever try to read the book with the sweat coming down your face and the woman screaming her bloody head off? We wanted the husband to do something. We turned around and he had fainted. He was a big help.

"'We'll have to get lots of hot water, Captain,' Norman said. 'Hot water. I

think you'd better get some more men out.' I said, 'Turn the whole bloody crew out, Norman, we got an emergency. Who knows, one of these clowns may have done this before.' Nobody wanted to have any part of it.

    "Anyway, out comes the baby. None of us were quite sure of that cord. It just said cut the cord. It didn't say, cut it here or anywhere. It just said cut it. Where the hell do you cut it? Where! Anyhow, we cut it pretty well close to the body and we got her into Rupert. That was out of my line completely. That was a frightening experience—a baby."

The *Cardena* returning from an upcoast voyage. Just visible is the bow of the *Lady Cynthia*, and the sterns of the *Lady Alexandra* and the *Coquitlam*.

    Clarence Arthur. Aboard the *Cardena* for years, Clarence Arthur was one of the senior chief engineers in the Union fleet. He had come to the company with the takeover of the Boscowitz Line. Arthur owned shares in Boscowitz, and it was widely believed he used this as leverage to get special treatment from the company. Not only was he the only chief engineer to have his own deck cabin, but he had his own table as well.

    A big, ham-handed man with a Buster Keaton face, Arthur was of one of those engineers who believed a ship's primary purpose was the safe transportation of the engine. He also believed engineers a superior class. He forbade junior engineers to talk with deck crews, and he would only grunt to captains. The sole exception to this was Capt. Robert Wilson, whom Arthur worshipped. When Wilson came aboard the *Cardena,* Arthur would throw his hands around Wilson's neck and embrace him.

    Arthur was so crabby it was widely thought he was Scottish. In fact, he was born in Nova Scotia and had learned much of his seamanship on boats working the Fraser River at the turn of the century.

    There was never any doubt about chief Arthur's feeling as to who was running things on a Union ship. On one occasion aboard the *Cardena*, the master called for more revs as they were bucking the tide through Seymour Narrows. The *Cardena* usually ran at 115 revs, so the crew member opened it up to the maximum, 120 revs. The Chief came down to relieve a junior engineer and he asked right away, "Who put up the speed of the engines?"

Chief engineer Clarence Arthur

"I did," said the engineer, "the skipper phoned me."

Chief Arthur shot back, "Don't ever do that again, young fellow. I'm the chief engineer. If they want more speed, they have to send me a note!" So Chief Arthur cut back the revs.

The skipper phoned down. "What in hell is going on?" he asked. "We're going backwards."

Chief Arthur folded his arms. "Don't answer them."

Pat Pattison

Pat Pattison. One of the senior Union pursers, Pat Pattison, or "Old Pat" was born in Australia in 1880. A tall, lanky fellow, given to gnawing on a pipe, he resembled an Oxford professor of mathematics. After almost every sentence, Pat said, "1, 2, 3, 4." When things got confusing, he said, "*E pluribus unum* and *dubious quim.*"

Pat liked jokes. At times when passengers were lining in front of the purser's office to get a berth, Pat would emerge from his room in civilian clothes, get in line, and start agitating the fellows to complain to the pursers about the bad service.

Occasionally a relaxed attitude to customers backfired. The *Cardena* had just pulled into Ocean Falls when a scruffy-looking passenger came aboard. Pat took a look at the man and said, "I've got no rooms; you will have to go in the steerage area."

The man said, "Do you know who I am?"

"No," said Pat, "and I don't care."

"Well," replied the man, "I'm Mr. Zellerbach." The purser's office on the *Cardena* had a blind at the wicket. When pulled down it read "Closed." As soon as Pat heard the name "Zellerbach" he pulled the blind down, poured himself a bracing slug of whiskey, then opened the blind and booked Mr. Zellerbach into the bridal suite.

Capt. Eddie Georgeson

Capt. Eddie Georgeson. "Captain Eddie" took over on the *Cardena* after Captain Johnstone went to the Pilotage. He was small (he stood on a stool while docking) and an immaculate dresser (his daughter ironed his handkerchiefs).

Captain Eddie was aboard the *Cardena* when it went through one of the worst storms to hit the coast. It was 1935 and the *Cardena* was southbound across Queen Charlotte Sound. The weather was unusually cold, and three deckhands had already suffered frostbite on the trip. The *Cardena* was being clobbered by immense waves. Tons of ice formed on the decks and the ship sunk deeper and deeper. A newspaper reporter of the day said the storm's "grim music sang overpoweringly of the trouble ahead" for the ship. Unable to turn the ship around, Captain Eddie wisely elected to put out the anchors. For twelve hours the storm raged and blew while the sleepless crew struggled to keep the superstructure free of ice. Finally, by Sunday morning, the storm abated and the *Cardena* was able to continue south. So good was the ship, boasted the captain in an article in the *Vancouver Sun*, that it survived the ordeal and made it back to Vancouver just twelve hours late.

Wee Angus McNeill

Angus McNeill. A slight, nervous man, with elfin eyes and a high forehead, "Wee" Angus, or "the Skye man" (he was born on the Isle of Skye), was one of the most superstitious of Union officers. Most Union navigators, like seamen everywhere, had some superstitions (no room 13 aboard, don't point at an animal ashore) but Wee Angus had a host of them. For instance, he would never steer a course with 13 in it, like N13W or N13E. Instead, he would call for N12 or N14. He didn't like to see priests or ministers aboard. He didn't like anything to do with dead people. When Capt. Neil Gray died, his widow gave Gray's new bridge coat to Capt. Harry Roach. Working under Captain Roach at the time, Wee Angus refused to enter the wheelhouse.

Over time, Union crews learned of Angus's superstitions, and took advantage of them. Knowing how terrified he was of bodies, the crew set up a pretext for him to come down into the lower hold to examine some damaged freight. They arranged to have one of their cohorts lie down beside a coffin and then sprinkled flour over his face.

Collisions between ships were rarely minor. The *Cardena*'s torn and crumpled plating is the result of a run-in with the tug *La Pointe*, in Goletas Channel, in 1942.

While Angus was poking down, the fellow let out a groan, then, like an apparition, rose up. All that could been seen of Angus was a blur going up the hold.

Despite his flighty nature, Angus had the ability to see a job through. Over the years, the company developed a system for handling cattle and horses. At the dock, the animal would be coaxed into a heavily reinforced box and a door would shut behind. This was the theory, anyway. In reality they did everything but what they were supposed to.

One time in Vancouver a horse steadfastly refused to go into the cargo box. The crew had failed and the mate, Angus McNeill, took over. While a crowd gathered, Angus pushed and heaved. Finally, the horse went in, but then reared up and its long front legs went over the front of the box. His Scots temper pushed to the breaking point, Wee Angus wound up and punched the horse in the nose. It reared up in pain, and came down with both legs inside the box. A cheer rose from the crowd and Angus swaggered off.

Capt. Bob Wilson. One of the calmest, most self-controlled of Union navigators, Captain Bob would amble onto the bridge of the *Cardena* before his watch, glance at the charts, and not consult them again for the duration of his watch.

The source of Wilson's reputation was his role in the sinking of the *Cowichan* on December 27, 1925. Under Captain Wilson, the ship was southbound out of Roberts Creek in a heavy fog when it was hit by the Union's SS *Lady Cynthia*. Realizing the *Cowichan* was in danger of going down before lifeboats could be lowered, Wilson ordered Capt. John Boden, on the *Cynthia*, to keep his engines at slow ahead, thereby plugging the hole. Wilson then assisted passengers and crew from the *Cowichan* onto the deck of the

Capt. Alfred E. Dickson

before following himself. "All right, Cap't," he hollered to Boden, "back her away before she takes us down with her!" Within moments the *Cowichan*'s bow rose out of the water and the little vessel slid, stern first, under the waves. Wilson looked at his watch. Eleven minutes had elapsed since the collision. "Well, that's it," he said. "Let's go below and have coffee."

Captain Wilson died aboard the *Cardena near* Quathiaski Cove, on December 21, 1947.

Two years after the *Cardena* was launched, the Union company ordered another combination freighter/passenger vessel for the northern runs. This ship arrived in BC in the spring of 1925 and was immediately put into service on the Prince Rupert–Nass River–Skeena River route.

The SS *Catala* was similar to the *Cardena*, except it had a promenade encircling the top deck—a feature that gave it a grandiose, liner-like appearance. It was also slightly shorter than the *Cardena* (218 feet to the *Cardena*'s 226.8) and had less cargo capacity (300 tons to 350). Both vessels were considered flagships of the company fleet. In its role, however, the *Catala* was very different from the *Cardena*. Whereas the *Cardena* was a flamboyant ship, with a flamboyant captain, the *Catala* was a more sedate, distinguished vessel. It was not the fastest ship in the Union fleet, nor the biggest, nor the most daring; rather, it was known as the best "feeder"—a term that referred to the actual food served as well as the civilized atmosphere on board.

This atmosphere, no doubt, had something to do with its skipper in the 1920s, the inestimable Captain Alfred Dickson. A weathered, blue-eyed sailor of the old square-rigger school, Dickson was the epitome of the staid, honourable mariner. He had no Christian name—it was always Captain Dickson. He never laughed out loud yet

Many Union employees thought the *Catala* the most graceful of all ships in the company fleet. Although similar in design to the *Cardena*, the *Catala* was a "stiffer" vessel and did not handle as well in heavy seas.

always had, as one observer said, "mirth" in his eyes. His sense of duty included the notion that his ship was to be a civil, safe place.

To many young residents of up-coast communities served by the *Catala*, Captain Dickson was the most worldly figure they encountered. Longtime Port Simpson resident Helen Meilleur once recalled how he tutored her through an early on-board romance. It was summertime, and while travelling north on the *Catala* Meilleur was befriended by a shaggy but attractive surveying engineer. After dinner, a Victrola record player and two scratchy records were set up in the ship's saloon. While the *Catala* made its way up the Portland Canal, toward Stewart, the two waltzed and fox-trotted late into the evening. At 1:30 a.m. Captain Dickson made a tour through the saloon. At 2:15 he made another turn, this time more slowly. At 2:45 he stopped in front of the dancing couple. They paused. Meilleur, flushed with confidence, told Captain Dickson that, as soon as the *Catala* docked at Stewart, she and the engineer were going to disembark and inspect the nightlife.

Captain Dickson looked the young engineer squarely in the eye. "I think Stewart's too rough for Helen at 3:30 a.m.," he ruled. "We're going down for a bit of supper before she turns in." Bidding the young man goodnight, Dickson held out his arm, bowed slightly and escorted Meilleur away to the officers' table. He ordered a slumbering steward to prepare a Union-style "snack." Out of spite, Meilleur recalls, she refused everything, including the famous Union pound cake shipped from Scotland.

The next day, while Dickson was easing the *Catala* into Port Simpson, Meilleur spotted the engineer talking to a blowzy redhead. Meilleur turned and gave Dickson her dirtiest look. He stared back. He usually growled his orders but this time, she recalled, he hollered. "Hold her hard astern!" Concluded Meilleur: "Our educations were the product of northern homes, southern high schools and the Union Steamship Company."

On November 8, 1927, the *Catala* was sailing south from Port Simpson to Prince Rupert. Captain Dickson was aboard, but chief officer Ernest Sheppard was on watch. Sheppard had opted to take the ship through the south Finlayson Channel, which was a more difficult but faster route than the frequently used northern channel. It was a clear day with calm seas.

Top: Crew of the *Catala* on boat drill. Union ships were involved in so many accidents that the wisdom of such exercises did not have to be impressed upon crews.

Above: A chief officer and quartermaster on the bridge of the *Catala*. Passengers were often invited to tour ships while en route.

Top right: Starboard view of the *Catala*'s clean lines. A distinguishing feature was the promenade which encircled the entire top deck.

The *Catala* in drydock, possibly after the Sparrowhawk Reef accident.

Port Simpson was a regular stop for the *Catala*. Union steamers started calling at the northern settlement as early as May 1897.

Capt. Ernest Sheppard

Chief officer Sheppard was, in almost every way, the opposite of Captain Dickson. A small, shrewish man, he seemed most intent on furthering his career. He was unpopular with Union crews principally due to his habit of consulting a higher power at critical moments. More than one quartermaster turned around to consult Sheppard during the heat of a storm, only to discover him down on his knees, praying feverishly. ("This thing kind of spoils your sense of security you know," remembered one quartermaster.) Once, during a heavy squall, an officer member was sent to summon Sheppard from his cabin. Sheppard was on his knees. "You get the hell up on the bridge," said the officer, "we need you more than God does!"

A few minutes before 1:00 p.m., as the *Catala* continued on its way south, Captain Dickson came into the bridge. In his hand he had a small watering can. He proceeded to the back of the bridge, where he tended a small window garden of pink geraniums and busy lizzies. Then, without warning, the *Catala* shuddered, and came to a grinding, metal-tearing halt.

Captain Dickson took over immediately. A quick recognizance indicated the ship was stuck, but not in imminent danger. Lifeboats were lowered, and a tug summoned. The forty-four passengers and most of the crew were transferred off and taken to Port Simpson, forty miles north of Prince Rupert. Captain Dickson and several engineers stayed aboard, in case the *Catala* might be refloated. But a dropping tide prevented that. The ship eventually keeled over to an angle of 45 degrees, and Captain Dickson gave the order to abandon the ship.

The *Catala* was stuck "hard and fast" on Sparrowhawk Reef for almost 30 days. Company officials were sure the ship's back would break when it was left dry at low tide.

Union ships were occasionally called on to transport the sick and injured to the R.W. Large Memorial Hospital at Bella Bella.

The *Catala*, it turned out, was impaled on the rock pinnacles of Sparrow-hawk Reef. Blocking the centre of Finlayson Channel, the reef was named after a British light naval cruiser that had gone aground there in 1874. The approach to the reef was supposed to be marked by a buoy, but there had been a terrible storm the night before and the buoy was dislodged. It had floated across the channel and become wedged in the reef. In the glaring light of midday, Chief Officer Sheppard hadn't noticed this and inadvertently used the buoy to navigate right up on the rock, one of those unfortunate but inevitable accidents that happened to every Union navigator.

At the inquest into the wreck of the *Catala*, however, Sheppard attempted to absolve himself completely of the affair. He said Captain Dickson was in command at the time of the accident. And the reason he thought this, he explained, was that Captain Dickson had come onto the bridge. To the crowd of Union employees and officials gathered at the hearing, Sheppard's statement was treasonous. Captain Dickson regularly came up to water his plants. He'd never taken over before; why would he now? It seemed like Sheppard was trying to destroy Captain Dickson's reputation to save his own—even when it wasn't actually on the line. But Captain Dickson would have none of it. With his white hair combed smooth and his clear blue eyes steady, he looked at the judges. He said, "Captain Sheppard thinks I took over. I guess I must have taken over." And that was all he said.

It was a dignified gesture that moved even the most hardened of sailors. With his experience, all Dickson would have had to do was challenge Sheppard and Sheppard would have been finished.

Meanwhile, the *Catala* was still stuck on the rocks. The problem was not that it was holed; rather it was held in a vice-like grip between two rock pinnacles. As the tide fluctuated between a high of 23 feet to a low of 7 feet, it threatened to break the ship's back. Several tugs, including the legendary *Salvage King* attempted to pull it off, but all were unsuccessful. With seasonal storms expected any day, the *Catala* was abandoned to the underwriters on November 14 with the unlikely proviso that if the ship could be refloated the company would buy it back.

Enter a grizzled old hard-rock miner. With no marine knowledge (he called the *Catala* a "bugger") he surveyed the situation and declared the ship could be saved if he was given a rock drill and a "little powder." He blasted the pinnacle jutting into the *Catala*'s hull, hoisted the debris up and out with the ship's winches, and over the ship's side. The hull was then patched and, on December 5, one month after it had ploughed ashore, the *Catala* was pulled off the rocks and refloated. It was towed to Vancouver and fixed at a cost of $175,000. On March 30, 1928, the *Catala* resumed her up-coast runs with Captain Dickson at the helm, both reputations intact.

Chapter Seven

1929-1935: Lady Alex and Cappy Yates

We are a marine community and love of the sea must be an inspiration in helping forward the destiny of our beloved city, so splendidly set in a wonderland of mountain and marine scenery.
Union Steamship Company brochure, c. 1931

The Union Steamship Company of BC endured losses during the Great Depression—services were cut back and office staff took as many as three pay cuts—but it weathered the era better than some competitors. Canadian National, for example. With the magnificent mistiming that became its trademark, CN launched three super-liners smack into the worst years of the Depression on the coast. The first of these, a sleek 384-foot three-stacker named the *Prince Henry*, went into service on June 21, 1930, running from Victoria via Prince Rupert to Alaska. It was followed soon after by the equally glamorous liners *Prince David* and *Prince Robert*. Not only was the economy in the doldrums, but these boats were too big for many coastal routes. Their short stay in BC was characterized by empty staterooms and echoing cargo holds. Within eighteen months the service was scotched: *Prince David* and *Prince Henry* were transferred to the east coast, and the *Prince Robert* was laid up for the duration of the 1930s.

There are several reasons why the Union company didn't suffer a similar fate. One was the death, on September 5, 1931, of company president Richard Welsford. The cheerful, duck-hunting son of J.H. Welsford, the man responsible for bootstrapping the Union company into a major concern in the years leading up to World War One, Richard inherited his father's puckered face (in photographs both look as though they've just eaten bearing grease), but little of his father's business acumen. One of Richard's first moves after

Opposite:
The busy Union dock illustrated graphically why the company was called the "up-coast streetcar line."

The amount of traffic on the coast couldn't warrant the extravagance of the Canadian National's palatial *Prince Henry*.

Union president Richard Welsford.

The *Chilliwack II*. As the *Ardgarvel* it had carried iron ore from northern Spain to the British Isles.

taking over as company president in 1922 was to sell off two ancient Union workhorses, the *Coquitlam* and the *Chasina*. Between them, these two ships had worked forty-seven largely trouble-free years for the company. In his zeal, Richard made the sale without securing guarantees from their buyers that the ships would be scrapped or employed elsewhere. The result was that the *Coquitlam* (under the name *Bervin*) went on to compete directly with Union vessels for fifteen years.

At the same time, Richard showed an inclination toward pricey new vessels. During his brief tenure, he presided over the launching of no fewer than six Union vessels, the last of which was the *Chilliwack II*, rebuilt from the British freighter *Ardgarvel* and launched in 1927. During the booming twenties, company coffers could tolerate this kind of outlay. Had the same trajectory continued into the 1930s, it could well have resulted in bankruptcy. With Richard's death, however, control of the company fell to trustees of the Welsford family, a timid bunch of teacup and doily types who insisted on a "no risks" policy. This turned out to be the best strategy for the Depression.

Above: The La*dy Alexandra* was licensed for 1400 passengers but often carried closer to 2000.

Left: On rare occasions when government inspectors, who travelled in pairs, tried to check passenger counts, Union crews put out a third and fourth gangway to throw them off.

Another reason the Union company survived the thirties was the enduring popularity of its excursion and day-boat operations. Of the five ships involved in this program, one ship in particular stands out. That's the SS *Lady Alexandra*, or, as she was known, the *Lady Alex*. Under the eccentric command of an elfin-faced, cigar-chomping master known as "Cappy" Yates, the *Lady Alex* regularly lugged overflowing crowds on excursions during the day, then carried similarly large crowds on moonlight cruises. Throughout the Depression, and in conjunction with the other Lady vessels in this fleet, the *Lady Alex* hauled hundreds of thousands of passengers (171,000 in 1937 alone), providing the company with a much-needed cash flow to offset losses on other routes.

The story of Cappy Yates and the *Lady Alex* is really the story of an entire division of the Union company. During the 1930s this division catered to Vancouver-area residents seeking a holiday, a getaway from the growing sprawl of the city. It became associated not with fist fights and bull blocks, but with the swish of skirts on a dance floor, peals of laughter, and late night buffets featuring hot drinks and pastries. If this seems a violation of the dominant images of the 1930s—gaunt-eyed rail-riders and Bennett Buggies—then it must be remembered that, even in the worst years of the Depression, 75 to 80 percent of the workforce was employed. These people had some money and, if they were fortunate, some holiday time. To them, the Union made an unbeatable offer: round trip to Bowen Island for one dollar, deal good until World War Two. For the generation of Vancouverites who could afford that buck, the Union Steamship Co. was the *Lady Alex* and Cappy Yates.

The Union company had always been interested in the tourist business. As far back as November 1889, the company's founders were noting the market potential. "The tourist travel, which is now very considerable, must rapidly increase," they observed in a prospectus, then lamented: "The want of a steamer adapted for this purpose, and excursions amongst the grand scenery…is felt during the summer months."

The company was to feel this "want" for three decades—mainly because its executives in those years devoted their attention to obtaining multi-purpose ships to supply the logging, fishing and up-coast community routes. If and when a cruise was needed in these years, one of the regular craft was used—under the creative description that passengers would be enjoying a voyage aboard a "working" ship.

Then, in 1917, the company moved into the resort business in a big way. In October of that year, it purchased the assets of the small, Vancouver-based All Red Line, including seven acres of land south of Sechelt known as Selma Park, and two steamers, the

An early attempt to cash in on the excursion business. Here the *Cutch* awaits while a party of excursionists picnics in Howe Sound. Isaac Oppenheimer, an early Union investor and director, is on far left.

Selma and the *Santa Maria*. The cost: $117,500. These two ships, originally built as private yachts (one, in 1881, for the Marquis of Anglesea, or the "Mad Marquis" who numbered among his on-board guests King Edward VII and actress Lillian Langtry) were renamed. The *Selma* became the *Chasina*, and the *Santa Maria* the *Chilco*.

The All Red Line purchase was followed by the acquisition, in December 1920, of the Terminal Steam Navigation Company. For $250,000, Union Steamships received two steamers, the *Ballena* and the *Bowena*, plus one thousand acres on Bowen Island, an idyllic setting about one hour's steamer service from Vancouver. Almost immediately work was begun to transform the property into a resort, complete with one hundred cottages, a dance pavilion and, in keeping with the company's obsession with things British, a model farm stocked with imported Ayrshire cattle. At the centre of the grounds was an imposing lodge, built in the shade of an even more imposing monkey tree.

To service this resort, the company set about creating a sub-fleet of ships designed almost exclusively for the day-trip and excursion business. These would be ritzier than the Union's usual vessels, and it was decided to give them the "Lady" prefix, to distinguish them from their more utilitarian sisters. (Most travellers knew them as the "Daddy" boats, because they brought working fathers to summer resorts on Friday evenings.) Several of these ships were conversions, the first being the *Lady Evelyn*, a twenty-two-year-old steamer famous for her rescue work (as the *Deerhound*) in the 1914 *Empress of Ireland* disaster. This was followed by the purchase of two former Royal Navy subchasers, the *Swindon* and the *Barnstable*. Designed for speed, not stability, these vessels were stabilized by the addition of sponsons. Relaunched, they became the SS *Lady Cynthia* and the SS *Lady Cecilia*.

Above: Like the *Chasina*, the *Chilco* was built as a yacht, in this case for industrialist John A. Rolls.

Left: The *Bowena*, formerly the *City of Nanaimo*, was renamed *Cheam* and ran until 1923.

The *Lady Cynthia* slipping under the shadow of Lions Gate Bridge. Capable of 15.5 knots, the former British submarine chaser was one of the Union's swiftest ships. Its cruising speed of 13.5 knots was faster than the top speed of many ships in the fleet. Tug in the background belonged to Coyle Navigation.

Above: Although designed as a multi-purpose vessel, the *Lady Alexandra* proved suitable only for the excursion business.

Left: Sponsors were added to the *Lady Cynthia* (pictured) and her sister ship, the *Lady Cecilia*, at the Coaster Construction Company's yard in Scotland.

At the centre of this fleet was the *Lady Alexandra*. Built in 1923 by the Coaster Construction Co. of Montrose, Scotland, the *Lady Alex* was designed almost exclusively for the excursion business. Among her distinguishing features was a promenade deck that ran three-quarters of her 225-foot length, and a hardwood floor extending the breadth of the ship, just over forty feet. Her restaurant, seating eighty-six, was the best equipped of any coastal steamer.

The *Lady Alex* arrived in Vancouver in June 1924, and immediately assumed the role of flagship of the excursion fleet. Whereas the other Lady ships showed the inevitable sutures and stretch marks from their former lives, the *Lady Alex* had pure, clean lines. Other Lady ships were powered by older, cantankerous engines given to belching black smoke, but the *Lady Alex* was powered by two new reciprocating, triple-expansion engines, capable of propelling the steamer through the water at a snappy 14 knots. It was a magnificent ship. Under a full head of steam, bunting snapping in the wind, there were few other vessels, Union or otherwise, that could match it.

Within months the *Lady Alex* also established that she had a strong personality. Although primarily designed for the passenger business, the ship also had a large cargo hold. Company officials had added this feature in hopes that each fall, in the wake of the summer excursion business, the *Lady Alex* might be put to use hauling cases of salmon from up-coast canneries. On her first trip north, however, the *Lady Alex* demonstrated she had no stomach for such work. Returning from the Skeena River, loaded with salmon, she hit rough weather in Queen Charlotte Sound. It was like loading the Queen Mother with shake blocks. The *Lady Alex* listed 35 degrees and threatened to roll over. She staggered back to Vancouver, the crew green of face. The company never let the *Lady Alex* that far north again.

In the role for which she was designed, however, the *Lady Alex* was perfect. While the other Lady boats handled smaller excursions to east Howe Sound ("Interesting ports of call are Britannia Beach, famed copper mining centre and Woodfibre, leading pulp

Left: *Lady Cecilia* and *Lady Alexandra* at Sechelt wharf

Below left: The Vancouver Waterfront Workers' Annual Picnic was always a riotous affair.

Below: Cruising at normal speed of about 14 knots, it took the *Lady Alexandra* an hour to get to Bowen Island.

and paper mill"), west Howe Sound, Sechelt ("Gulf Coast Riviera") and Savary Island ("one of the loveliest island gems on the north Pacific Coast"), the *Lady Alex* whisked hundreds of holidayers to Bowen Island, or on special excursions to Victoria, or up the Fraser River to New Westminster. This was the era of the company picnic, and the decks of the *Lady Alex* were often crowded with employee outings for BC Electric, Kelly Douglas or Woodwards. Twice a week, in summer, the *Lady Alex* ran moonlight cruises to Bowen Island.

When it came to Bowen Island, the company's brochure writers pulled out all the stops. It was a "Lovely Isle," a "Happy Isle," a "Wonder Isle"; it was "Pleasure Garden," "Marine Playground," a place where the "Spirit of Recreation reigns supreme."

Attempting to keep a ship running under these conditions was hard work. The crew showed up at 7:00 a.m. to begin loading mail and freight. On return, cargo and mail had to be unloaded and the ship thoroughly cleaned, which took until 7:00 or 8:00 p.m. On picnic days and dance cruises, quitting time for the crew would be as late as 1:00 a.m.—making for a sixteen- or seventeen-hour day. The deck crew were paid $69 per month. Not much, even for the 1930s.

Understandably, staff turnover was very high. The quartermaster, winchman and dayman were the only permanent employees. The rest of the deck crew was made up of students and waterfront drifters.

In addition to their regular duties, the crew were expected to maintain order on a ship with up to two thousand partying passengers. The most difficult time was often on the return journey from Bowen Island to Vancouver. Something happened at Bowen Island: people left their brains there. At midnight, the ship's whistle would signal to passengers on shore that it was time to reboard. Whereas the loading in Vancouver was an orderly affair, reboarding was a circus. As many as five gangplanks were used, and the crush of people was staggering. Standing at the top of the gangplank, pursers and assistant pursers were supposed to take tickets; in reality they grabbed at anything offered. After the ship was

By 1935, Bowen Island was one of western Canada's best known resorts. Thousands flocked to it, via the *Lady Alexandra*, each summer.

loaded, this mess of paper was thrust into the purser's office, to be counted and sorted. Among the items found were BC Electric streetcar transfers and a Chicago hat shop stub.

This trip back to Vancouver was a riotous time. One fellow would often climb over the ship's bow railing as she backed out, then dive, fully clothed, and swim back to the wharf. Usually there was a dance band on board and they would go up to the bridge as the ship was leaving and play "Aloha" or "At the End of A Perfect Day." One drunk did a swan dive from the dance floor railing onto the dining room below. Couples ducked into any available nook or cranny. When Union crews discovered a couple under the wooden covers of a lifeboat, they bolted down the covers and left them until the ship arrived in Vancouver. People became sick and vomited, or depressed and cried. One man tried to kill himself. On another occasion, a woman crawled out underneath the bridge and got stuck. She was left there until the ship docked since the officers thought it too dangerous to rescue her while the ship was moving. One captain had searchlights mounted, and as the *Lady Alex* passed under the Lions Gate Bridge he would turn on the lights and announce through a bullhorn: "OK folks, time to end all the love-making." Back in Vancouver, crew had to lug drunks off the ship and stack them, like cordwood, on freight dollies.

Lording over this chaos on the *Lady Alex* for many trips during the 1920s and '30s was Capt. Billy Yates. A small, wiry man with exceptional jug-handle ears, "Cappy" was admirably suited to the *Lady Alex*.

Billy Yates's own career resembled a series of excursions. Born in the town of Llanfairechan, Bangor County, North Wales, on May 23, 1889, he was indentured at age eleven to a veteran captain. In return for teaching young Yates seamanship, the Captain received fifty pounds. Yates was with this captain for two and a half years, signing off on October 26, 1903. The next day he signed on board the *Lake Manitoba*, a steam freighter sailing to Montreal. After the *Lake Manitoba*, Yates served aboard six deep-sea ships of the Canadian Pacific and White Star Lines for four years, the last one being the *Cyclops*, sailing to

Capt. Billy Yates was master on seven Union vessels, including the *Lady Evelyn.*

Japan and the west coast of North America. While the *Cyclops* was in Tacoma in March 1907, Billy Yates jumped ship. In a letter, the chief officer of the *Cyclops* noted that although Yates had "deserted" ship, he had "proved himself sober, and attentive to his duties." After the *Cyclops* came a series of hip hops that saw Yates bouncing from the Union Steamships, to the CPR, to the Grand Trunk Pacific, back to the Union company, then to the Marine Navigation Co. and back to the Union, where he was to stay until he retired in 1957.

Yates was a capable, if not outstanding, mariner. Of several minor accidents during his career, the most notable was in 1919, when he distinguished himself by ramming a US warship. Yates was master aboard the SS *Britannia* at the time, a worn-out little steamer belonging to the Marine Navigation Co. He was taking the *Britannia* out on her final voyage. With a full load of passengers, he cruised into Vancouver harbour where the giant battleship USS *New Mexico* was anchored. After observing the ship for a few minutes, Cappy gave the order to back away, or go astern. For some reason never fully explained, the ship jumped forward. It hit the *New Mexico* with a resounding crash. High above the *Britannia*, US sailors leaned over the edge of their ship and laughed. One cupped his hands and hollered, "Try again, Captain, and we'll see if *Britannia* rules the waves." There was more guffawing. As Cappy moved away, the sailors broke into a rendition of "Rule Britannia."

Captain Yates on the deck of the *Lady Alex.*

Aboard the *Lady Alex*, Cappy Yates had his own set of rules—often at variance with those of the company. The company insisted on ship limits, but under Captain Yates, the *Lady Alex*, licensed for fourteen hundred passengers, sometimes carried two thousand. The company also wanted ships to arrive and depart on time. Captain Yates arrived and departed when he felt like it. Once he even held up an entire ship so a crew member could retrieve a child's hat.

The *Lady Alex*, docked at Bowen Island, had just blown her departure whistle. Immediately a child on the boat deck began to howl. It seems a gust of wind had blown his hat off into the water of Snug Cove, where it floated some yards from the ship. Cappy turned to his quartermaster. "Go and get that kiddie's hat," he said. The

Top: Aircraft of the 1920s and 1930s couldn't carry enough cargo or passengers to seriously challenge the Union's role as the primary mode of transportation on the coast.

Above and right: Vancouver *Sun* columnist Penny Wise once called the resort at Bowen Island a "gigantic romp."

Left: The *Lady Alexandra* arrived in BC with a ballast of sand from Scotland's east coast. The sand was discharged, via barges, onto beaches of Deep Bay, on Bowen Island.

Below: For its Diamond Jubilee, celebrated during the week of July 1, 1949, the Union company hired celebrities such as Betty Phillips and Thora Anders from Vancouver's Theatre Under the Stars to perform aboard. At the time the Union fleet consisted of 16 passenger and freight vessels.

quartermaster knew the first rule of seamanship, namely that you don't argue with a captain. He ran down to the dock and over to the boat float, where he was fortunate to meet Howard Hines just tying up his fourteen-foot clinker-built "putter." Hines knew the quartermaster,

Passenger deck on the *Lady Cecilia* or *Lady Cynthia*.

and let him borrow the boat. He picked up the child's hat on first pass, receiving a huge cheer from the crowd on deck of the *Alex*.

Cappy Yates understood instinctively that being captain on a ship like the *Lady Alex* had as much to do with showmanship as seamanship. He was a dapper dresser and, at critical times, would steam on a dirigible-sized cigar. Behind the scenes, though, he was fantastically absent-minded. One of the more solemn duties required of masters is the depositing of cremated remains overboard and the recording of the event in a ship's log. It's a responsibility probably dating back to the era of four masters. For Cappy Yates, it was one more thing to get in the way of a pleasant cruise.

On one occasion, while having a drink in his cabin with another officer, Yates slopped booze into a glass and remarked, "See that little box over there on the settee?"

The box contained someone's ashes, to be sprinkled into the sea when they reached Point Atkinson.

Capt. Eric Suffield

The two men sat around and talked, then all of a sudden Captain Yates dashed out with the box, up to the wing of the bridge. He did his duty, then fired the little box after the ashes. He came back to the cabin, saying, "Well that's that. Now I must remember to enter the name in the logbook." His face dropped. "Oh my God," he said, "what was his name?"

Cappy ran a smooth ship. The only problems he had were with Union management. Rightly, they suspected him of being a heavy drinker. It was said among crew members that Cappy Yates could hear the cork coming out of a bottle anywhere on the *Lady Alex*, and get there before the first drops were poured. In their efforts to catch Yates out, Union officials kept a special eye on him, so he couldn't get bottles aboard. Yates got around this by having quartermasters, outfitted in special windbreakers with deep pockets, make the dash to the Carrall Street liquor store before boarding.

Cappy only came close to getting nabbed once. That was when coming into the Union dock after a particularly boozy trip. Among those gathered on the dock were several officials, including Eric Suffield, the shore captain known as the "Sea Beast." The Sea Beast had been out to get Cappy for some time and suspected Cappy might be cut. From the dock, it seemed as if Cappy had only two choices: take the boat in himself and risk a crack-up, or stand back while his chief officer did the docking, and face an explanation later. But Cappy was a clever man, and soon came up with option three. Leaving his chief officer inside to dock the ship, he went out onto the bridge, to pose with a second set of controls. The ship slid into the dock like a hand into a glove.

The relationship between Cappy Yates and the *Lady Alex* lasted throughout the 1930s and '40s—the heyday of the excursion business. By 1951 the cruise and excursion business was falling off, a result of an increasing fascination with the automobile for holiday transportation and an improved highway system. At first, the *Alex* was

only put into service for the summer. Then in 1952 she was withdrawn altogether. Several years later, Cappy retired. After sitting in mothballs for seven years, the *Lady Alex* was purchased by a group of Vancouver businessmen, and in 1959 the ship was converted into a floating restaurant near the Bayshore Inn. Captain Yates was the guest of honour on opening night. Once a month for several years, Captain Yates would journey from White Rock for a morning visit to *Lady Alex.* On each of these occasions Cappy would be asked to stay for lunch; he always declined.

On February 14, 1966, while cleaning his son's swimming pool, Billy Yates slipped and drowned. He was seventy-six. His funeral notice declined flowers. The staff of the landbound *Lady Alex* asked for an exception, and it was granted. Apart from the family's observance at Cappy Yates's funeral, there was one wreath: "From *Lady Alexandra.*"

Bowen Island residents marked the time of the day by arrival and departure of the *Lady Alexandra.*

Chapter Eight

1935-1949: From Purge to White Boats

Opposite:
The former Canadian
National ship *Prince
Charles* was renamed
Camosun II. Although
its accommodations
were outdated, the
ship served well
during World War II on
the Queen Charlotte
Island run.

> Salal bush. Stump ranch.
> Floatcamp. Chokerknob.
> Rockcod. Net float.
> Steampot. Store boat.
> Camp boat. Mission boat.
> Fishin boat. Union boat.
> **Raincoast Chronicles**

Three events marked Union company history between 1935 and 1949: a fractious strike in 1935; the arrival of a new ship from Scotland several years later; and the purchase of three surplus warships in 1945.

Spring 1935 saw the Union company readying the fleet for another busy summer season. Day-boats, laid up for winter, were stocked and supplied, while up-coast vessels were pulled from regular schedules and scrubbed from stem to gudgeon. Brochures were printed; the resort at Bowen was prepared. It was a hectic time, all geared around one date, May 24.

Just as the nine o'clock gun marks the passage of the day in Vancouver, the May 24 sailing of the Union fleet marked the passage of the years. The day-boat fleet, ornate in bunting and gleaming under new paint, would sail out of Vancouver harbour, past crowds gathered at Brockton Point. Officers used the occasion to swap the drab black hats of winter for crisp white summer ones. It was a celebration to mark the departure of the grey days of winter and early spring, and to greet another summer on the coast.

On May 24, 1935, however, there was no celebration. Although the fleet had been readied, a strike was called at the last minute, and the excursion ships remained tied

The strike of May 24, 1935 shut down Union service. Vancouver residents said it was the first time they'd seen every ship in the fleet in port at one time.

Capt. John (Jack) Boden started his career aboard Fraser River sternwheelers.

up at the Union dock. Initially, the strike concerned problems specific to Union vessels. But within weeks the whole waterfront was out on strike and the company and its employees were plunged into a bitter confrontation that was to last more than six months.

To this point in its history, the Union company had managed to avoid serious labour problems. There had been a brief series of strikes in 1917, 1919 and again (also on the May 24 weekend) in 1920, but these were small affairs and didn't disrupt service. Generally, the company had demanded and received a high degree of loyalty from its employees. Also, many Union seamen had come off ocean-going sailing ships, and accepted any on-the-job deprivations in stride as part of life on a ship, Union or otherwise. If there was a grievance, it was settled between crew and captain. Like the time on the *Chelohsin* when the crew threatened to not wash or shave unless a shower was installed. The captain of the day, John Boden, took the matter to the company and within a week the *Chelohsin* was outfitted with a shower.

By the mid-1930s, however, that thinking was changing. This was the era of worker activism, and downtown Vancouver street corners and Union halls rang out with calls for the working man to unite against the exploiting capitalists. Represented by the Seafarers Industrial Union, the Union crews demanded a change in basic working conditions—especially for crews on up-

Union purser Art Twigg riding a board of liquor out of the hold of the *Catala* at Dawson's Landing, Rivers Inlet.

coast vessels. Work on these runs could be brutal. Often up-coast vessels carried coal for the canneries, and after that was unloaded, the salmon was loaded on top. Salmon at the time was shipped in wooden boxes containing 96 half-pound cans. It wasn't unheard of to load

Deckhands had to find time between stops to keep the ship's gear in order.

5000 cases at a stop. They were either loaded with winches through cargo holds, or through the side cargo doors. This was a tricky job, navigating dollies loaded with crates of salmon over sagging gangplanks. In the hold of the ship, boxes were stacked two and three high, by the thousand. While officers, quartermasters and watchmen had specific hours of duty, deckhands were required to work long hours. In the Skeena River, where canneries were close together, it wasn't unusual for crews on such runs to work thirty-eight hours straight. Furthermore, these ships often returned to Vancouver late. This lost time was absorbed by the crew's time off; it wasn't unusual for a crew member to have just a few hours at home before having to return for another week at sea.

One week after it had begun, the May strike was over. Initially, it looked as though the employees had won major concessions from the company, which had agreed to grant the workers their principal demand—that the twelve-hour day be replaced with a nine-hour day. It also agreed to change the practice whereby second mates did the hiring, and to give one day off per week.

But Union crews returned to work only to find themselves on strike two weeks later. This time they went out in support of longshoremen in Powell River. With sides deadlocked, Union vessels remained in port. After a time, with police protection, the company got crews together and managed to get one or two boats out. Eventually a whole ghost crew was formed, and the company bought in two ships as housing.

While the company returned to work, regular Union crews languished at

Above: The Union office at the foot of Carrall St. In the company's heyday, loggers used to hang around the wharf to catch up on the most recent gossip from upcoast camps.

Right: Deckhands, like officers, stewards and engine room staff, kept to themselves.

home or stood around the Hastings Street soup kitchens that had been set up near the Union docks. Times were so tough, only crew members could use the soup kitchens—not their wives or children. With no strike pay and zero chance of finding work elsewhere, the strike unravelled. Six months after the whole thing started the strike was over. Those employees whom the company liked were given their jobs back, although some suffered demotions; those they didn't like never worked aboard Union ships again.

Following the end of the strike, it was the Union company's turn to move against the workers. This was known as "the Purge." Over the years Union employees had come to accept as part of their job the perks of running a black market aboard the ships. The company discovered this while checking the purser's list of passengers versus the actual number of passengers coming down the gangplank. There were more passengers than listed, indicating that the pursers were selling tickets and pocketing the fare.

Further investigation revealed a whole list of scams. A favourite purser's trick was to charge a drunk for meal tickets knowing he'd soon be passed out or too busy partying to eat. The purser would then resell the meal tickets to another passenger and pocket the change. Another trick was to stuff a laundry bag full of roasts and cheeses and expensive food and unload it at a dock. It would be returned with a bottle or two of booze. In one case, Union officials discovered a company purser was paying off travelling prostitutes with turkeys and hams stolen from company supplies.

Deckhands had their scams too. Through careful mismanagement of cargo, they always had contraband to sell—sugar, wool socks, pants. Boom chains were another valuable commodity. The standard price for a boom chain off the back of a Union ship was four dollars, cash. Up-coast crews used to sell whiskey. Poured into a pop bottle and stopped with a cork, it sold for one dollar. All this activity was carried on from the back of the ship, usually in the early morning.

The Purge lasted until 1938. It resulted in a number of senior company pursers losing their jobs. Coming on the heels of the failed strike, it also had the effect of demonstrating to company employees who was in charge.

Ships are intriguing machines. Launched as metal envelopes, stuffed with cylinders, pipes, shafts, bearings, tanks, bulkheads, pumps and instruments, they become, at some point in their career, more than the sum of their parts. When this metamorphosis takes place has been the subject of many a whiskey-fuelled mariners' argument: the moment a ship slides off the shipbuilder's ways? During the first encounter with heavy seas? Or is it a slow evolution, formed from years on a run, where steady service is the measure of character?

The character of Union ships was developed, generally, over several years. Thus the *Cassiar* became known as a "lucky" ship, the *Cardena* "happy," the *Catala* "gracious," and so on. Other company ships, though, identified themselves through a single event. Such was the case with the *Lady Rose*.

The *Lady Rose* was built for the Union company in 1936, at the A & J Inglis Point-house Shipyard in Glasgow. (It was originally named *Lady Sylvia*, but, as was the case with the *Cariboo*, it had to be changed after another ship of the same name was found to be already in operation.) It was a small ship, comparable in size to the original *Comox*. But it was important symbolically because it marked the end of the company's self-imposed austerity program.

The *Lady Sylvia*, renamed *Lady Rose*, was launched from the shipyards of A. & J. Inglis, Ltd., Glasgow, Scotland, in 1937.

With its open upper deck seating, the *Lady Rose* qualified for a summer licence for 130 passengers. Her winter licence, however, was for 70 passengers, which severely limited its use.

The *Lady Rose* arrived in Vancouver on July 11, 1937, after a two-month, stormy journey across the Atlantic, through the Panama Canal, and up the West Coast. (The captain's last log entry reads "Vancouver, Thank God.") Within days it was put into service on the West Howe Sound route. Its captain was Jock Malcolmson and the chief engineer was Bobby Travis. During an early trip to Britannia Beach, the crew of the *Lady Rose* finished loading the last of a small band of passengers and Captain Malcolmson rang down for standby. This was standard practice on Union ships to ensure the engineers were ready to depart.

But this time there was no response. Captain Malcolmson tried again. Still nothing. He sent a deckhand to investigate. The man found Travis hanging by the neck in the engine room. He had committed suicide. The death, predictably, gave rise to a rumour, and rumour imbued the ship: there was a ghost aboard. For years afterward crew were reminded of the chief engineer whenever an engine room door lock malfunctioned and the door flew open. Whoever was on watch would say, "Oh, there's Bobby coming up."

The arrival of the *Lady Rose* also presaged the largest ship-buying spree in Union history. In the eighteen months after Canada's declaration of war, in the fall of 1939, the company bought no fewer than eight vessels. Most of these came with the purchase of the Frank Waterhouse Company, an established coastal freight carrier whose black-funnelled vessels sported a distinctive "W" on a star laid over a white circle. Included in the deal were the freighters *Northholm*, *Southholm* and *Eastholm*, plus three chartered vessels.

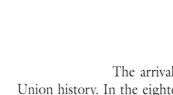

With a cargo capacity of 1100 tons, the *Southholm* was the largest of the three vessels purchased with the takeover of the Frank Waterhouse Company. Also included in the deal was the *Bervin*, which the Union had sold as the *Coquitlam* in 1923.

All of them were aging. The *Northholm*, for example, had been built in 1924 and by 1940 its best days were past. Pressed into wartime service hauling pulp, the ship carried on until 1943, when it was caught in a fierce gale off Cape Scott, at the northern tip of Vancouver Island, and sunk. All but two of the seventeen-man crew were killed. Recalling the incident later, one of the two survivors, chief officer Ray Perry, said the heavy sea simply opened the plates of the old single-bottomed freighter.

The Waterhouse purchase was followed by the acquisition, in June 1940, of two medium-sized Canadian National steamers, the *Prince Charles* and the *Prince John*. The *Prince John*, renamed the *Cassiar II*, had been built in 1910 for the Grand Trunk Pacific.

Left: Although the *Cassiar II* was aging, it operated almost continuously during World War II. It could make the run from Vancouver to the Queen Charlotte Islands in about 48 hours.

Below: Armour plating was added to the *Camosun II* and the ship was painted camouflage grey.

Launched as the *Amethyst*, it had served with the GTP until the company went into bankruptcy in 1916, then sailed under Canadian National colours. Although slow (maximum speed 11 knots), the *Cassiar II* was a good sea boat. It had a passenger licence for eighty-five, including thirty-eight cabin berths, and could carry four hundred tons of cargo.

The other CN vessel, the *Prince Charles*, was renamed the *Camosun II*. Like the *Prince John*, it was a multi-purpose ship, although it was a sleeker, faster ship, and indulged the convenience of passengers, having a capacity for 178 passengers and 150 tons of cargo. The *Prince Charles* started out as the *Chieftain*, running the Glasgow–Storno-way route in northern Scotland for the David MacBrayne Fleet before World War One. In 1919, it was sold to the Orkney and Shetland Steam Navigation Co. and re-named the *St. Margaret*. In 1925 it was sold to Canadian National and went into coastal service in 1926.

Like the core of the Union fleet, these new vessels underwent a wartime facelift. Armour was added to the bridge and the hulls were painted dull grey. Anti-torpedo devices were added to the hulls, trailing the ships like fishing gear from a troller. Attempts were even made to arm the ships. The first of these was the *Camosun II*. It was docked and a large gun mounted on the aft deck. On the day the gun was to be tried, the ship was boarded by a large contingent of career navy officers, who according to a crew member had "gold braid up to their elbows." They sailed into the Strait of Georgia, and prepared to fire the gun. Officers and crew members lined the decks. A command was given, and there was a tremendous crash. The recoil was so great that all the light fixtures in the dining room smashed to the floor. A layer of pre–World War One dust rose, then settled on everything. Clearly, the old ship wasn't up to battle standards.

But the *Camosun*'s saga wasn't over. Limping back into Vancouver harbour, the crew forgot to fly the proper wartime identification flag. There was a signal station under the Lions Gate Bridge and all ships entering the harbour were supposed to show their identity—*Camosun* included. Never mind that the ship was falling apart at the rivets; the Army needed its identification. The whistle of a well-aimed shell overhead was the first indication for the *Camosun* and its cargo of dignitaries that something was wrong. The sound sent crew scrambling to hoist the proper flags, while the navy brass sent their own signal by lining the decks, indicating the *Camosun* was not an enemy ship.

At the root of such comic scenes, however, was a real sense of danger. Japanese submarines were known to be off the coast, and it was only a matter of time before one struck. Then, in late June 1942 it actually appeared as though a submarine had sunk a Union boat. According to front page stories, a vessel named the *Camosun* had been torpedoed in local waters. They didn't mention exactly where, or when, because of news blackouts. To Union staff in Vancouver the loss seemed impossible. A Union boat torpedoed?

The Japanese submarine I-26, sister to the I-25 that torpedoed the Fort Camosun.

Their worries were short-lived. Several days after the story ran in the papers, the *Camosun* bumbled innocently into Vancouver harbour. The ship's crew were oblivious to the reports of their demise, until they saw the crowd gathered at the company dock, waving and celebrating. The attack, as it turned out, had been real. But it was a Liberty freighter named *Fort Camosun* that had been torpedoed. That vessel's name had been virtually unknown on the coast because of the information blackout. The *Fort Camosun* was sailing from Victoria on its maiden voyage on June 19, 1942, carrying a cargo of plywood, when it was spotted near Cape Flattery by the Japanese submarine *I 25*. Although damaged the *Fort Camosun* managed to struggle to a nearby port.

War changed the face of the Union fleet, but aboard the ships life went on much as it had for the past fifty years. Life on a Union ship, like life in a logging camp, was hard and simple, but in many ways very good. Crews had a specific job, and when they did it they were done. No families or other distractions in their off-hours.

At the centre of on-board life was food. Food was the real perk of a Union job. Smart crew members struck deals with cooks. A pair of wool socks would get you a

month's worth of special pancakes, stacked like a pyramid, or all the deep-dish apple pie they could eat.

The menu from the *Cassiar* for December 25, 1942 was an example of how the Union company stoked their crews' fires:

Cream of Oyster soup. Grilled fillet of salmon maître d'hotel.
Fried fillet of mignon with mushrooms. Roast young turkey & sage dressing.

The Union tradition of fine dining survived the war. The *Coquitlam II* featured a club style dining room that seated sixty.

Inevitably, booze figured largely in the daily life on board. During the war, when liquor was rationed, it was difficult to get a drink. If there was a layover in Campbell River a crew member might be able to hoof it to the Willows or the Quinsam. But they had to be quick because as soon as bartenders heard the ship's whistle they closed shop, saving supplies for locals.

Another trick was developed for getting liquor across the border at Hyder, just across the Alaska–BC border from Stewart. Perched on the border was an American customs office. In the winter, amid ice and snow and cold weather, the officer would look out a little Dutch window and ask if a traveller had anything to declare. One Union crew member bought two bottles and tied them to a long piece of string, one at each end. He then wrapped the string around his waist and folded his coat over top. When the customs man asked if there was anything to declare, the crew member said no, and was waved on. The

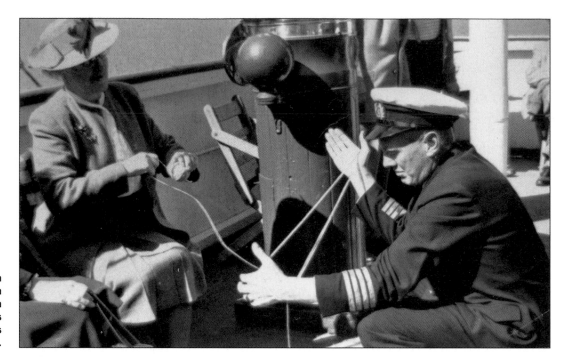

Capt. Harry Roach served on Union vessels from 1917–1958. He was popular with crews and passengers alike.

customs man shut the door and the bottles clunked along twenty feet behind.

Pranks were another feature of daily life. On the *Lady Pam*, a favourite trick was to catch seagulls by opening one of two adjacent portholes and offering a piece of bread. When the gull came down, another crew member reached out the second porthole and grabbed the gull. Released inside, it flew around creating havoc. Another trick was to foul up another crew member's routine. Pat Pattison used to hang his beer bottles out his porthole so they would reach perfect quaffing temperature. On one occasion Denis Shaw noticed them and, while the *Cardena* was in dock, removed the bottles, poured out the beer, and urinated in them. Pat never hung out his beer again.

Crews, like that of the original *Cassiar*, presented a rough exterior, but were fond of practical jokes.

Cadavers were also used in practical jokes. Over the years, Union vessels carried dozens of bodies, usually from up-coast logging camps to Vancouver for autopsy. In

the early days, these were simply put in a box on deck, covered with a blanket and employed by off-duty crew as a card table. Later, in an attempt to keep the body from decomposing, the coffin was stored in a lifeboat.

Wally Walsh invented one of the more ingenious pranks. One lunch hour he came bouncing into the officers' mess and announced, "I've finally got something I've wanted for years. I just have to show you fellows." From his pocket he extracted a tiny box and removed the lid. Lying in a bed of bloodied cotton batting was a finger. It was a trick, of course, but it spun the stomachs of a few green officers.

Like private school students, everyone had nicknames. Some, like "the Skye Man" (aka Angus McNeill) took their names after their birthplaces. Others, like Dave "Broken Nose" Franklin, took their names from facial features (caused, in this case, by a German rifle butt). Officers tended to have grandiose names: Robert Ashmore was "The Black Prince," Harry Biles was

"Hurricane Harry," John Halcrow was "The Viking"; although there were exceptions: Jack Calderwood was "Flannel Foot" and Joe Hackett "Mouldy Joe."

Deck crews, on the other hand, had nicknames that reflected their job: "Big Pete," "Big Mike," "Cowboy," "Springline," "Red," "Suitcase" and enough "Blackies" to man a ship. The stewards, who were thought by the rest of the crew to be slightly effeminate, had a different sort of name: "Daddy," "Dinty," "Teddy," "Scotty" and the infamous "Titch," who was given to reprimanding over-particular crew by whanging them on the head with a dinner plate.

Aboard ship, crews tended to make friends with people of the same rank. Officers would play cards and trade books with other officers, while deckhands did the same. One of the most enduring friendships was between William "Big Bill" Aylward and "Little" Dick Bridsen. Big Bill was a hulk of a man, over six feet tall and capable of driving a marlin spike into the deck of a ship with such force than no man could remove it except him. Little Dick, on the other hand, was a slight man with diabetes.

Big Bill and Little Dick were winchmen on the *Catala* for years. They shared a room. Bill was a bachelor and lived at the Patricia Hotel. Dickie was married and had six children. Their friendship dated to a labour dispute in 1935, when Union ships were run for several months by scabs. Dick Bridsen, with his large family to support, could not afford to be on strike. So Big Bill escorted Little Dick through the picket line. Years later, when Little Dick became ill, Big Bill saw to it that Dick's family was looked after.

Then there were relationships that can't be characterized as "friendship" but nonetheless were significant. Captains and quartermasters often developed this sort of bond through hours on the bridge together. Such was the case with Gus Ericksen and Captain Roach. Captain Roach liked Gus because he was a capable quartermaster, not prone to excitement. For his part, Gus liked working with Captain Roach, because Roach had no sense of smell and Gus was in the habit of showing up at work dead drunk. Gus used to tell everybody that he never caught a cold because his system was so full of alcohol a germ couldn't get a foothold. Further, he said he kept Captain Roach healthy because he was always breathing over him.

Two well known Union officers.
Left: Jimmy Galbraith and Harry Roach

War had been hard on ships and men. Many captains and company officials had been run ragged trying to keep up with demands. The war had been particularly hard on Captain Muir. As shore captain, he was responsible for stretching the over-taxed, aging fleet. After the war, Muir developed a case of hiccups that lasted four months.

By this time it was obvious some of the company's older ships would have to go. Among the first to be sold was the *Camosun II*. In August 1945 it was purchased by the Oriental Navigation Co. of Tel Aviv, Palestine, for $77,000. Under the name *Cairo*, it carried immigrants to the Holy Land and routes throughout the Mediterranean until 1950, when it was laid up and, two years later, scrapped.

Another vessel to go was the *Venture*. A key in the company's up-coast service for thirty-five years, it was sold to a Chinese business concern in September 1946. Renamed the *Hsin Kong So*, it was damaged by fire at Honolulu on November 12, 1946, then destroyed by another fire at Hong Kong on February 2, 1947.

As part of a plan to upgrade the fleet, the company's management decided to purchase three Castle Class corvettes from the War Assets Corporation. Initially the deal seemed a good one. The sleek, swift craft were available for $75,000 apiece, a fraction of what it would have cost to build a new vessel. The company could invest a lot of money in rebuilding the warships into classy liners and still come out in the black. With coastal cargo markets declining, it was anticipated the "White Boats," as they were to be called, would pick up new business in the expanding cruise ship business.

The first of these ships to arrive was the former HMCS *Leaside K492*. Built in England in 1944 as the HMS *Walmer Castle*, it had been transferred to Canada for use in the North Atlantic. During the winter of 1945 the ship was rebuilt. Cabins were added, as were cargo handling facilities. It was during this time that the first hints of trouble with the new ships appeared. Under the original plan, the company would spend just under half a

Right and below: Delays in the conversion of the corvette HMCS *St. Thomas* to the *Camosun III* resulted in the ship missing its first scheduled season.

million dollars per vessel on upgrading. Those figures soon went out the window. With unexpected costs, the final price was closer to three-quarters of a million dollars.

During rebuilding, the company invited several senior skippers to visit the ships. One of these was Capt. John Boden, a curmudgeonly old employee known for his jaunty cap. Captain Boden was touring the bridge when he spotted something strange. It was a gyro compass, an improvement on the magnetic compasses with which older Union vessels were equipped. "What the hell is that?" snarled Boden. A crew member working on the renovations explained politely that it was a gyro compass—a superior instrument to the old magnetic compasses. Boden was unimpressed. "Get that damn thing out of here. I won't have that aboard my ship."

The ships' reputations went from bad to worse. As soon as they were launched it became apparent they guzzled fuel at a greater rate than old Union steamers like the *Cardena*, yet could carry only half as much cargo. The *Cardena* and the *Catala* were both twin screw ships and were easy to manoeuvre in tight bays and inlets up the coast. The Castle type corvettes were single-screw so the company installed bow rudders to make them

Left: The *Camosun III* heading up Observatory Inlet enroute to Alice Arm. Engine smoke was so thick that deckhands had to hose down aft seating areas before passengers could go outside.

Below: Hopes that the White Boats would usher in a new era for the Union company were abandoned within several years of their introduction.

Opposite page top and bottom:
The refurbished *Coquitlam II* had
to be eased through the False
Creek railway bridge before it
could be put into service.

Left: The *Camosun III* at Alice
Arm. Constant scuffing against
docks left the white boats looking
shabby. They were then painted
conventional black.

Above and left: Not only were the new ships ill-equipped to handle large cargo, such as vehicles, but they made life difficult for traditional Union navigators such as Capt. Jack Boden.

more manoeuvrable. The *Coquitlam II* and the *Camosun III* were delivered to the company with bow rudders. But they were virtually useless as they were operated manually, slow to activate and slow to disengage. On the first drydocking the bow rudders were sealed and their machinery removed.

Another innovation that didn't work out was the deepening of the stern and the addition of a skeg on the bottom of the hull. Besides reducing speed, this mass of metal also disturbed the water flow to the propeller. This in turn just increased fuel costs. On the *Chilcotin* the added framework set up such a horrendous vibration in the stern that the whole thing broke away from the hull.

Further problems were discovered on the *Coquitlam*'s sea trials. The ship's funnels were too short. When these "white boats" were first commissioned, their funnels were short, squat, streamlined and pleasing to the eye—but not too practical. When steaming full out there was a tendency for the funnels not only to leave vast quantities of soot all over the aft deck but also to burn lifeboat covers. One of the chores of the midnight to 4:00 a.m. watch was to administer vast quantities of steam up the funnel to get rid of any unnecessary soot and grime. This work usually took place at about 1:00 a.m. Later in the morning the deck crew would wash down the decks and boat covers before passengers stirred. The funnel problem was later corrected with the addition of a six-foot metal extension on top of the funnel. At the same time the hull was painted black to conform to the rest of the USS fleet.

The white boats, it seemed, could have an obnoxious streak in them. The *Coquitlam*, under John Boden, was heading into Butedale to pick up a load of frozen and canned fish. Landing at Butedale was tricky because of a waterfall that created turbulence near the dock. If the ship was not going fast enough the stern would swing out before reaching dock. On this occasion Captain Boden brought her smoothly alongside the dock, as he usually did. But it was necessary to move the ship ahead to load the frozen fish. Captain Boden was on the bridge and rang down for "slow ahead." Instead he got "slow astern." Panicked, he rang for "full ahead." The ship lurched backwards even faster. Something was wrong. Fred Smith, the chief engineer who should have been down below at the throttle, was up on the deck, watching the move. Captain Boden saw him and yelled at him to get below, but by now it was too late. Somewhere along the line, the engine room did get an "ahead" order from someone below and the ship flew ahead. It crashed into the ice shed, and the ship's lines—which were all cable—broke and were whipped around dangerously. Timbers were landing up on the bridge. A big hole was gouged in the wharf. When the ship was able to back away, one of the shed's windows was stuck on the bow of the *Coquitlam*. It was, in short, a terrible mess.

By 1949 even the company was convinced the corvettes, or "White Elephants" as they were now universally known, were only useful for summer tours. During the winter they were boarded up. That left the Union's aging warhorses—the *Catala*, *Cardena* and *Chelohsin*—to carry the brunt of traffic.

Chapter Nine

1949-1958:
The Union Founders

Founder, to, the act of a ship which sinks at sea, generally understood to be by the flooding of her hull either through springing a leak or through striking a rock. Other causes of a ship sinking, such as an explosion, etc., are not usually associated with the word.

The Oxford Companion to Ships and the Sea

At approximately 7:40 p.m., Sunday, November 6, 1949, the Union steamer *Chelohsin* rounded Point Atkinson and set a course ESE for the company docks in Vancouver. It was returning from Lund and Savary Island with a near-capacity load of passengers. Outside, a patchy fog obscured the city lights, and the vessel proceeded cautiously.

On the *Chelohsin*'s bridge, Capt. Alfred Aspinall and several officers peered ahead and discussed the best approach. The First Narrows, they knew, could be treacherous in the dark. Their task was complicated by the fact that the ship's radar had quit several hours earlier, while leaving Lund. At one time this wouldn't have presented a problem, as Captain Aspinall would have navigated with the ship's whistle. Since radar had been installed, however, he had gotten out of touch with the time-honoured technique and was unsure of using it.

At first Aspinall wanted to take the *Chelohsin* into English Bay and wait until the fog cleared. Then he changed his mind and decided to try easing the ship in anyway. An officer on the bridge suggested he use the ship's phone to contact the radar station on Lions Gate Bridge. It could help the *Chelohsin* in. But Aspinall didn't go for that, either. "I've been coming in here long before there was a bridge," he said.

It was to be one of the most important decisions in Union company history.

Moments later there was a thump, and the *Chelohsin* jumped and came to a lurching halt. At first crew members thought the *Chelohsin* had run over a log boom. But it

Opposite:
At one time the whole town of Port Hardy would have turned out to greet the Union boat. By 1947 roads and aeroplanes had cut into the company's business.

Right and below: The inconvenience of losing the *Chelohsin* was compounded by the fact that it was salvaged by an amateur.

wasn't logs the ship had hit; it was some rocks 100 yards off Siwash Rock. The *Chelohsin*'s bow had run over several large boulders, one that had punctured the metal plating near the aft.

Orders were given to abandon ship. While some of the crew scrambled to lower life rafts, others rounded up the passengers, many of whom were unaware of the severity of the accident, and prepared them for emergency off-loading. Most complied, but one woman had caged chinchillas aboard she didn't want to abandon. Crew members tried to talk her into leaving the animals, but she was adamant. They had to go, too. The crew acquiesced and the chinchillas were loaded into a lifeboat. There the animals caused further trouble, because their crates made it difficult to navigate. The lifeboat eventually made its way to shore, at which point the woman had the nerve to insist the chinchillas be lugged up to the road.

Over the next several days Union officials crawled through the old steamer, trying to determine whether it could be salvaged. It didn't take them long to decide. It was a write-off. Backed by the advice of waterfront experts who said the *Chelohsin* could never be refloated, the company put it up for sale on an "as is" basis. On November 24 it was purchased for $1600 by Victor David, a businessman. David, who owned David Neon, was an amateur salvager. After consulting with a former engineer on the *Chelohsin*, he hired two tugs to pull the wreck off the rocks and into the Evans, Coleman, Evans dock, near the Union dock. It was then resold for $25,000 to a San Francisco scrap dealer, who had the ship towed out of the harbour. Pat Keatley, marine editor at the *Vancouver Sun*, penned the epitaph. "They humiliated her," he wrote, "they dragged her backwards through the First Narrows to die."

In many ways, the fate of the *Chelohsin* foreshadowed the fate of the Union company. Stuck with an outdated mode of transportation and an outdated way of thinking, the company bumbled its way through the 1950s before coming to a ignominious end.

By this time the competition did not come so much from other shipping companies, as from aircraft. Forward-thinking entrepreneurs like Jim Spilsbury were running flights in and out of camps all over the coast. For only a slightly higher fare, a logger could be off the side of a hill and in town in hours, instead of days.

The advent of the good, reliable outboard motor also had an impact on Union business. With an outboard, the operator of a small camp could make a quick dash to town, or to run in a crew from the end of a dirt road. These men didn't need the Union ships.

Against a backdrop of bigger changes, the Union company staged its own drama. Under the control of the Welsford family and, as of the late 1930s, the CPR, the company had been encouraged to provide thorough local service. That changed in 1954 when a group headed by Senator Stanley McKeen acquired a substantial interest in the company. This group came up with some fantastically hare-brained schemes—all of which were antithetical to the Union's traditional role. One of the worst of these plans—based on

The *Chelohsin* hung up on some rocks 100 yards west of Siwash Rock off Stanley Park.

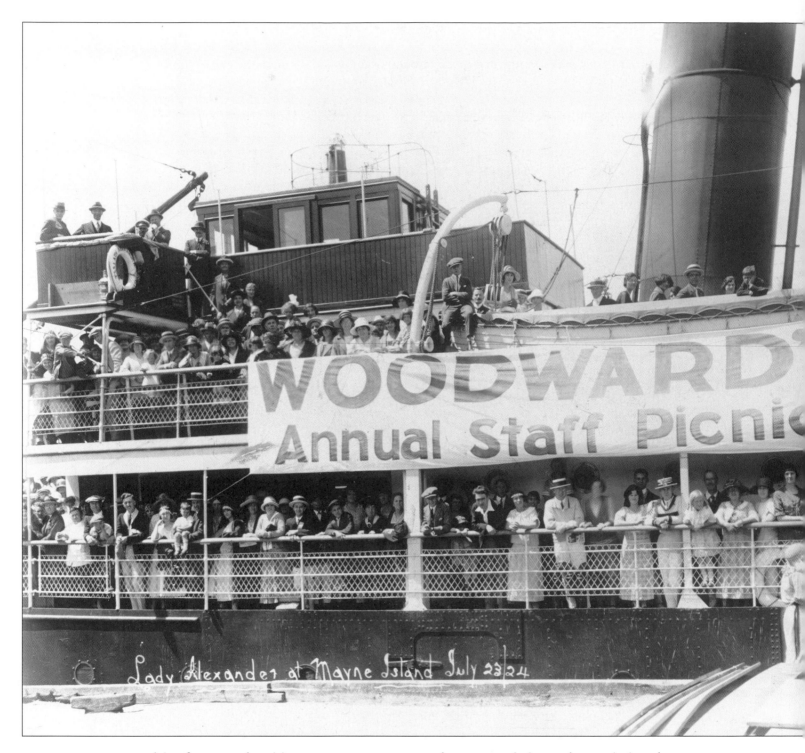

advice from an advertising man—was to revamp the company's image by repainting the corvettes. They emerged in a putrid combination of pastels. One trip up the coast and they were the laughingstock.

Another plan was to revamp the company estate on Bowen Island. In 1956 it was announced that millions of dollars were to be spent transforming the slumbering Bowen Inn and environs into a swanky international resort that would, said Senator McKeen, "have an important bearing on the flow of tourist dollars to BC." Buildings and cabins were to be levelled and replaced. It was to be renamed Evergreen Park Resort. The resort was a flop, abandoned even before it was finished, and the Union managed to alienate most of the island's population. Not only did the company go to the unheard-of length of charging islanders admission, but in its enthusiasm for washing itself of its own image it cut down the much-loved monkey puzzle tree in front of the hotel.

Far left: At Mayne Island in 1924, the *Lady Alexandra* shows the popularity of the Union's excursions. However(at left and below), the company's attempt to make the Bowen Island operation into an international resort didn't go over well with locals, who stayed away in droves. They liked the Union the way it was.

A similar attitude was evident in the company's approach to dealing with employees. Under old management, Union had let employees work until they couldn't make it up the gangplank. Not so the new company, which hacked and slashed in a fashion that would have pleased many corporate henchmen in the 1980s.

One of the first to go was Harry Biles. "Hurricane Harry" had been with the company since 1928, working his way up from quartermaster on the *Catala* to the senior position of shore mate. On June 29, 1956, he received the following letter:

As of the 1st of July 1956 the position of Shore Mate will cease to exist, you will thereafter be employed as rigger at an hourly rate of $2,00 and will report to the machine Shop Foreman for orders. You will punch the time clock and fill in time sheets. The other shore gang and three watchmen will fill in time sheets as at present done by the regular Machine Shop crew. The work will be carried out on a job number basis.

Kindly instruct your crew accordingly.
(Signed) Thos W. Morgan
Supt. Engineer.

And Harry, it turned out, was one of the lucky ones. Many older Union employees were simply let go. Like Freddie Smith. He was aboard a Union ship in Prince Rupert when he received a wire from the company's Vancouver office. Smith, it said, was being retired, effective on his return to Vancouver. He would receive $60 per month. This was the first Smith had heard about his impending retirement. Such treatment served only to wedge the company and crews apart.

The mood on Union steamships was so depressing that it seemed to affect the vessels. The *Cardena*, flagship of the fleet for years, and still an excellent ship, underwent a character change and took to ramming into rocks. Starting with a grounding on the Capilano River in March 1952, it went on to crash into a rock in Sullivan Bay in early 1953,

Even the flagship *Cardena* needed assistance in the 1950s.

then collide with the CPR's *Princess Elizabeth* in October 1953, and go aground at Duvall Point, near Port Hardy, in November 1956. It even set a company record of sorts, piling up twice in one day.

And so it went through 1957 and 1958, a pattern of bumbling and mishap that, as up-coast observers could see, must come to an end. Still, when it came, the end was a shock. On January 14, 1959, it was announced the Union company had sold its fleet to Northland Navigation Company, an energetic upstart headed by Capt. H.J.C. Terry.

For Gerald Rushton and others of a literal mind, this was the end of the Union company. For those men who worked and ate and slept aboard the vessels, however, the closure seemed artificial. They could take a Union ship out of service, and even sell it, but it was at heart always going to be a Union boat. Thus in the years after 1958 we watched as the *Lady Alex* was transformed into a restaurant; then, after being towed to California, a nightclub called Dirty Sally's. In the same way we observed the demise of the *Cardena*, as it was auctioned in 1959, then towed to Kelsey Bay, where it was sunk as a breakwater for a log booming grounds.

In 1990 the *Lady Rose*, still in active operation, journeyed from Victoria to Vancouver to help celebrate the one hundredth anniversary of the Union Steamship Company.

And in the same way we still watch the career of the *Lady Rose*. The only Union ship still in active service, the *Lady Rose* continues to ply the waters of west Vancouver Island to Barkley Sound, still carrying the ghost of Bobby Travis, freshly painted and rarely, rarely late. The *Lady Rose* sails as the spectral legacy of the Union Steamships and the men who found their way aboard.

Appendix I

Union Steamship Co. Personnel, 1920–1958
Note: Names have been compiled from ships' registers and oral history sources; therefore, some spellings may be incorrect.

Masters, Chief Officers and Mates
Ashmore, Robert "The Black Prince"
Aspinall, Alfred "Uncle Alfie"

Biles, Harry "Hurricane Harry"
Boden, Jack, Sr. "Handsome Jack"
Browne, John H., Sr.
Browne, John R. "Buster"

Calderwood, J.M. "Flannel Foot"
Campbell, Donald M.
Campbell, Neil
Charters, Tom
Coles, H. George
Corneille, F.E. "Cornie"
Crowles, Byron F.

Dickson, Alfred E.

Farina, Denis
Findlay, James
Freisen, Irving J.

Gaisford, George
Galbraith, Jimmy
Georgeson, Edward
Gilbert, F.W.
Godfrey, Lorne A.
Gray, Neil
Green, Stanley

Hackett, Joe "Mouldy Joe"
Halcrow, John J. "The Viking"
Hamer, C.A. Charles
Hannigan, M.J. "Paddy"
Hayman, V.D. "Vic"
Horne, John "Johnny"
Hosken, Geoff
Hunter, James "Jimmy"

Johnstone, Andrew "Andy"

Kelly, Harvey
Kennett, Bill
King, Leonard C.

Lamacraft, Harry
Lawrey, Howard E.
Lewis, Charles "Charlie"
Lucas, Thomas M. "Tom"

McAskill, J.A.
McBeath, Robert P. "Bob"
McCombe, William, Sr. "Billy"
McCombe, William, Jr.
McIntosh, Dave
McKillop, James
McKinnon, A.J.
McLean, Henry C. "Harry"
McLeod, J.
McLeod, John M. "Pop"

McLennan, A., Jr.
McLennan, A.C., Sr. "The Rajah" or "Big Mac"
McNeill, Angus "Wee Angus" or "Holly Saints"
McPhee, J.D.
Malcolmson, John I. "Jock"
Marette, Billy Jan
Mercer, John
Morrison, Don
Morrison, Iain
Mounce, William W.
Muir, John "Jock"

Naughty, R.T., Sr. "Bob"
Naughty, Robert, Jr.
Nicholson, William "Nick"
Noel, James E.

Owen-Jones, Bertram G. K. "Curley" or "Alphabet Jones"

Park, John
Parker, Fred "Searchlight"
Perry, Ray W.

Reid, Alex
Roach, Henry "Harry"
Robinson, Miles "Robbie" or "Gigli"

Scanlon, "Paddy"
Seymour, R.
Sheppard, Ernest M.
Smith, Bob
Smith, C.B.
Spry, Bill
Stewart, Jim
Strang, A. "Al'"
Suffield, Eric W. "The Sea Beast"
Summerfield, J.E. "Slim" or "Anxious Moments"

Thompson, Bob

Walker, Joe
Walsh, A.E. "Wally" or "The Baron"
Warden, Bill
Watt, James
Whitehurst, George
Williams, J.W. "Chips"
Williamson, Robert "Bob"
Wills, Ralph
Wilson, Angus
Wilson, Robert "Bob"

Yates, W.L. "Billy"

Engineers
Annan, Tom
Armour, James
Arthur, Clarence

Bain, Iain
Baldry, Robert
Beattie, Andrew "Andy"

Cahill, Al
Calbeck, Fred
Capewell, Tommy
Carpenter, Jack
Catchpole, C.

Chadwick, C.T. "Chad"
Craigen, George
Croucher, George

DeGrouchy, A.
Dick, Thomas M. "Tom"
Douglas, J.

Emms, Ernie
Emms, Reg

Farina, Patrick J.V. "Paddy"
Fisher, Johnny
Fletcher, Alex
Foster, George H.
Francis, James "Jimmy"

Gilligan, John
Goddard, George
Granquist, Edward
Gregory, Robert "Bob"
Green, Jimmy
Grieves, James "Jimmy"

Halliday, Sam
Hill, Jack
Hogan, John
Hunt, John C.L.
Hunter, John

Jefferson, Lancelot

Kando, Bob

Liston, Walter
Logan, Robert
Lyall, Jimmy

MacAuley, John
McCormick, Clarence "Abe"
MacDonald, Hugh
MacGregor, Duncan
MacKenzie, R.G.
McLean, Don
McLean, James "Jimmy"
McLelland, Davie
McLeod, Angus "Jock"
McQuarrie, E.
Mackie, William
Main, Boston "Jimmy"
Marrs, George
Matheson, Fred
Mattock, Edwin A.
Miller, J.
Millier, Cecil E.
Munro, Jack
Murchant, Michael
Muskett, Larry

New, Oswald J. "Sparky"

Paterson, Bill
Pope, William

Scott, Ned
Shugg, Gordon
Smith, Ben "Benny"
Smith, Fred Edward "Freddie"
Spencer, Tommy
Steele, Andrew "Andy"
Stein, Robert A.

Strand, Bob

Travis, Bob
Turnbull, W.
Tweddie, Napier

Vince, Gordon

Whitelaw, Robert "Bob"
Whiteman, Bill
Widdess, Jack
Williamson, W.
Wishurt, William

Pursers, Assistant Pursers and Freight Clerks
Anderson, Clarence Alan
Anfield, Sidney
Anthony, Harvey
Atkinson, Jack

Barrowclough, C.W. "Joe"
Beaton, Raymond
Benson, Michael "Mike"
Berry, William A.
Bigger, Roger
Billingsley, Jim "Bo Bo"
Bourne, Herbert A.
Boyd, William M.B.
Braddick, Harry J.
Brynant, Leonard E.

Chapman, Hugh
Charters, David
Coates, E. Darrel
Coldwell, Gordon
Coldwell, Randle
Collier, Ernest J.
Conk, Arthur
Cook, Gordon P.
Crompton, Harold N.

Dean, Morris
Dudley, Leonard A.
Dutka, Henry "Hank"

Enwright, Eddie

Finlayson, Ron
Finnson, John F.
Foote, Gerry
Fordyce, George "Lonesome George"

Gerrard, John
Gill, Henry "Harry"
Goody, Fred
Green, Herbert
Greig, George
Guy, Charles "Charlie"

Hale, Stuart J. "Stew"
Halliday, Ian
Halford, A. Cedric
Hartford, Harold
Hatchen, Anthony Thomas "Tom"
Hooven, Danny
Hughes, H.A. "Pinky"
Hunter, Stan

Ives, Harry

Jones, Gerry

Kelly, Joe "Little Joe"

Lannard, H.B.
Lawrence, Frank
Lawrence, Kenny
Lucas, Michael "Mike"

McCue, Philip "Phil"
McElroy, Neil
MacKenzie, Vernon F.
McLean, Sidney "Neil"
McLeod, Don
Miller, Norm
Moore, James A.
Morlock, Neil

Nelson, Don
Newman, Al
Nogarr, Frank O.

Parsons, Leslie L.
Pattison, Norman G. "Pat" or "Paddy"
Perrott, Dennis
Pickerill, F.
Price, Lloyd
Procopio, Richard S. "Dick"

Rankin, William "Bill"
Rannie, Gilbert, "Gibb"
Read, George R.J.
Richmond, James
Robinson, Amos W. "Robbie"

Shaw, Denis "Danny" or "Denny"
Showbridge, George W.
Showbridge, H. "Bert"
Simms, John
Skinner, Frank Jess
Smith, Bert
Smith, Les
Smith, Russell M.
Spence, G.
Stanfield, Jack
Stewart, Jerry
Stockland, Egolf
Storey, Jack
Stover, Reginald C. "Reg" or "Smokey"

Tozer, Allan H. "Hugh"
Tracy, Steve "Dick"
Twigg, A.M. "Art"

Vanantwerp, Stanley
Van der Werff, Richard "Dick"
Victor, Bill

Walker, R.W. "Bob"
Waters, Bob
Watts, E.
Williams, Clarence
Williams, J. Wensley
Williams, Ozzie
Wood, Norrie
Wooster, H.J.
Wyllie, Patrick

Youdon, Ivan

Chief Stewards
Archers, J.
Attewell, Albert "Bert"
Audley, Harry

Booth, G.T.

Cummings, "Scotty"

Davidson, Norman
Deschner, G.

Ebden, Bert

Gardiner, William "Willie" or "Daddy"

Hartley, Jack
Holdgate, Clarence C. "Slim"
Humphreys, Harold

Innes, D.

Keen, Harry
Knight, Alfred "Bogey"

Lanches, C.

McDonald, Hugh "Little Mac"
McEwan, William H. "Bill"
McGregor, J.
McGuiness, "Dinty"
Main, Dickie
Minnes, John J.

Pickerall, Fred
Scotter, Edwin I. "Teddy" or "Red"
Short, Albert
Singleton, David
Skinner, Walter

Tripp, Jack

Watts, Ernie
Wycherley, C.
Wyllie, Patrick

Deck Crews
Allan, John
Allin, Clinton
Allin, Doug
Anderson, "Smokey"
Andriani, Frank
Anger, George
Annan, Tom, Jr.
Arnett, Jimmy
Aylward, William "Big Bill"

Barron, Stan
Barry, Roy, Jr.
Bartlet, Geoff
Beck, Stan "Buddy"
Berg, Alfie
Best, Daulfred "Joe" or "Doffie"
Boden, Jack, Jr.
Borden, Alex
Bridsen, Dick "Dickie"
Brown, Dennis "Brownie"

Brunt, Cliff
Bunker, Bert
Burkmar, George "Barnyard"

Cahill, Tommy
Cambell, Dave
Cambie, Ormand
Campbell, Malcolm
Charleton, Alex
Coles, Bob
Cooper, George
Corson, George
Costigan, Ed
Cushing, Les

Daisely, Neil
Darby, Ken
David, Frank
David, Prosper
Davidoff, Bill "Molotov"
Draper, Len
Dumont, Freddie
Duncan, Laurie
Dwyer, Paddy

Eaton, Dean
English, Dickey
Ericksen, Gus
Estey, Bill
Everly, John

Farley, Walter
Flager, John
Fletcher, Ken
Foote, Dave
Fraser, Jack
French, Al
French, Wally
Frenchy, "Paper Nose"
Frieson, "Squeak"
Fry, Bill

Gammon, Bill "Squeeks"
Geisburg, Billy
Gerbrandt, George
Gibson, Ernie
Gibson, Gib
Gourlay, Henry
Gowdy, Johnny
Greenlaw, D.
Grens, Stan
Grisenthwaite, Dan
Gurley, Henry

Hacayway, Brothers
Hageman, Norm "Slim"
Haines, Al
Hanke, Kelly
Hansen, Mark
Harper, George "Scotty"
Harris, Bucky
Harwood, Johnny
Hildich, Paddy
Hill, Albert Jr.
Hireen, Bill
Holbrook, Phil
Hornsby, John
Hotra, George
Husband, Gus
Hynes, Kenny

Jamison, Don "Scotty"
Jensen, Magnus
Johansoon, Ole
Johnsen, Ed
Jones, Davie
Jones, Gibb
Jones, Gordie
Jones, Ivor
Jones, Len
Jones, Percy "Blighty"
Jorgenson, "Blacky"

Kelly, "Bum Mitt"
Kelly, "Suitcase"
Kendall, Adam
Kennet, Bill
Kennet, Fred
Kennet, Ted
Ketchum, Bill
Ketchum, Fred
Kristchuk, Nick

Lawson, Bill
Lawson, Ray "Blackie"
Lucas, Ernie
Lyons, Al

MacAulay, Malcolm
McEwan, Dick
McEwan, William H.
McFadden, Ed
McGuiness, "Springline"
McIntosh, Dave
MacKenzie, John Angus
Mackie, Scotty
McLean, Robert "Bob"
McLeod, Jack
MacLeod, John
McLeod, Rod
McLeod, Scotty
McMeekin, Tom
McMillan, Johnny
McNalley, Jimmy
McNiven, Dan J.
McPherson, Norm
Manning, Ben
Martinson, John
Merrer, Alex
Michael, Percy "Big Mike"
Michaluk, Albert "Red"
Middleton, John
Miller, Jimmy
Mirkly, Red
Morrissey, Pat
Mowat, Doug
Muirhead, Jack
Musgrove, Gil "Squeek"

Nelson, Nels
Nicholson, Danny

Obrecht, Chick
O'Donnell, Jimmy
O'Rivers, Penty
Owens, Johnny

Page, Charlie
Park, Colin
Patton, P.M. "Big Pete"

Plant, Ernie
Prendergast, Al

Rand, John
Rees, Melvin
Reid, Alex
Reid, George "Bucky"
Renwich, Ricky
Rinder, Don
Rive, C. Elliot
Roach, Edward "Ed"
Roach, Will
Robertson, Scotty
Rosi, Don
Ross, Alan
Russel, Phil

Satchwell, Dave
Scott, Bill
Senvoich, Steve
Seymour, Ralph
Simmons, Arnie "Cowboy"
Smith, Alan
Smith, Boyd T.
Smith, Doug J.
Smith, Joe
Smith, John
Smith, Stanley A.
Smith, Steele
Solem, Ed
Spence, "Scotty"
Spry, Bill
Stanley, "Chuck"
Stanley, Ned
Stephens, Charlie
Stephenson, Keith
Stevenson, Don
Stevenson, Johnny
Stewart, Roy
Stewearton, Fred
Storey, Doug
Strachan, Charlie
Suffield, Neil
Swanson, Harry

Taylor, Sid
Thompson, Ken
Thompson, Lorrie
Tite, Ted
Tovash, Johnny "Tiny"
Tufts, Wally
Turner, Al
Turner, Jack

Vanderdike, Johnny
Verge, Rod
Vincent, Carl

Waldon, Jimmy
Walker, Johnny
Watson, Jimmy
Watt, Jimmy
Watt, Wally
White, Jackie
Williams, Al
Wilson, Bud
Wooten, George

Young, Gordon

Appendix II

Union Steamships Fleet, 1889–1959
Total number of vessels: 53

Argus
In Union service: 1950–1953
Type: Steel tanker motor vessel. Built as the *Y-30* for the
US Navy in 1944 by Kyle & Co. at Stockton, Calif.
Purchased from Pacific Petroleum Co. as the *Argo* and
renamed *Argus*.
Dimensions: Length 157.3', breadth 27.2', depth 19.9'.
Gross tons 517.
Engines: Diesel. Speed 10.5 knots.
Services: Carried liquid petroleum and dry cargo.
Capacities: Cargo 800 tons. Tanks for 200M gal. liquid
fuel.
General: Burned at Ioco, BC, on June 15, 1953.
Converted into transport barge by Straits Towing Co. in
1954.

Camosun I
In Union service: 1905–1936
Type: Steel passenger–freight vessel. Built by Bow
McLachlan & Co., Paisley, Scotland, in 1905.
Dimensions: Length 192.7', breadth 35.2', depth 17.9'.
Gross tons 1369.
Engines: Triple expansion 224 NHP; two boilers
cylindrical multi-tubular. Speed 14 knots maximum.
Services: Prince Rupert and northern BC ports.
Capacities: Passenger licence 199, berths 68, deck
accommodations 120. Cargo 300 tons.
General: One of the company's most powerful ships.
Pioneered route to Prince Rupert. Retired in 1936 and
scrapped.

Camosun II
In Union service: 1940–1945
Type: Steel passenger–freight vessel. Built 1907 in Ayr,
Scotland, by the Ailsa Shipbuilding Co., as the *St.
Margaret* for the North of Scotland and Orkney &
Shetland Navigation Co. Renamed *Chieftain*. Later
operated by CN Steamships as *Prince Charles* on Queen
Charlotte Islands service. Bought and renamed by Union.
Dimensions: Length 241.7', breadth 33.1', depth 11.1'.
Gross tons 1344.
Engines: Single, triple expansion, 257 NHP. Speed 13
knots.
Services: Wartime operation between Vancouver, the
Queen Charlottes, and Prince Rupert.
Capacities: Passenger licence on Queen Charlottes route
150, otherwise, 178. Cargo 150 tons.
General: Sold in 1945 to Greek owners and renamed
Cairo.

Camosun III
In Union service: 1946–1958
Type: Steel passenger–freight vessel. Built 1943 by Smith's
Dock Co., Middlesbrough, Eng., as Castle-class corvette
HMS *St. Thomas*. Converted 1946 by Burrard Dry Dock
Co., North Vancouver, BC.
Dimensions: Length 235.7', breadth 36.6', depth 22.5'.
Gross tons 1835.
Engines: Triple expansion, IHP 2800. Speed 15 knots
maximum.
Services: Northern BC, including Queen Charlottes; later
several seasons in Alaska cruise service.
Capacities: Passenger licence 200, berths 114, deck 16.
Cargo 250 tons.

General: Name changed to *Chilcotin* after sale of that
vessel in February 1958. Sold in June 1958 to Alaska
Cruise Lines and renamed *Yukon Star*.

Capilano I
In Union service: 1891–1915
Type: Steel screw freighter–passenger vessel. Hull
prefabricated in sections by J. McArthur & Co., Glasgow.
Launched from Union shipyard in Vancouver's Coal
Harbour in 1891.
Dimensions: Length 120.0', breadth 22.2', depth 9.6'.
Gross tons 231.
Engines: Bow McLachlan & Co., Paisley, Scotland.
Compound 28 RHP. Speed 10 knots maximum, 8.5
average.
Capacities: Passenger licence 25 (increased during
Klondike gold rush). Cargo 300 tons.
General: Struck rock near Texada Island September 30,
1915, sank off Savary Island October 1, 1915.

Capilano II
In Union service: 1920–1949
Type: Wooden single-screw passenger–freight vessel. Built
1920 at BC Marine, Vancouver, BC.
Dimensions: Length 135.0', breadth 26.9', depth 8.2'.
Gross tons 374.
Engines: Inverted, direct-acting, triple expansion, NHP
51, built 1914 for the steamer *Washington*. Speed 13.5
knots maximum.
Services: Operated on Sunshine Coast–Howe Sound
routes.
Capacities: Summer passenger licence 350, winter 150.
Cargo 50 tons.
General: Retired 1949.

Capilano III
In Union service: 1951–1959
Type: Steel cargo motor vessel. Built 1946 at Port Arthur
Shipyard Co. as *Ottawa Mayferry*, and later named *City of
Belville*. Renamed *Capilano* and dieselized after Union
purchase in 1951.
Dimensions: Length 145.0', breadth 27.1', depth 8.0'.
Gross tons 530.
Engines: Diesel BHP 400. Speed 12 knots maximum.
Capacities: Cargo 500 tons.
General: Renamed *Haida Princess* by Northland in 1959.

Cardena
In Union service: 1923–1959
Type: Steel twin-screw passenger and cargo vessel. Built by
Napier & Miller, Old Kilpatrick, Scotland, in 1923.
Dimensions: Length 226.8', breadth 37.1', depth 18.4'.
Gross tons 1559.
Engines: Direct-acting, triple expansion, IHP 2000. Speed
14 knots maximum, 13 average.
Services: Weekly on cannery route to Skeena River, also in
Bella Coola–logging camp service.
Capacities: Passenger licence 250, cabin berths 132. Cargo
350 tons; refrigeration for 30 tons boxed fish; carried
11,000 cases of canned salmon.
General: The Union's finest sea boat. Sold in 1961 to
Capital Iron and Metals Co., Victoria, BC. Hull was resold
and sunk as breakwater in Kelsey Bay.

Cassiar I
In Union service: 1901–1923
Type: Wooden passenger–freight vessel. Built 1901 at
Wallace Shipbuilding Co., False Creek, Vancouver, using
hull of the *J.R. McDonald*, a schooner launched in 1890 at
Ballard, Washington.

Dimensions: Length 120.6', breadth 29.0', depth 6.9'. Gross tons 597.

Engines: Bow McLachlan direct-acting, inverted surface condensing, one multi-tubular boiler, single-ended amidships. Speed 9 knots.

Services: Logging camp routes.

Capacities: Passenger licence 144, cabin berths 42, also open berths in loggers saloon. Cargo 110 tons.

General: Most famous of all Union ships. Sold to Seattle interests in 1925 and transformed into a dance hall on Lake Washington.

Cassiar II

In Union service: 1940–1949

Type: Steel passenger–freight vessel. Built 1910 by Scott & Sons, Bowling, Scotland, as the *Amethyst*. Brought 1911 by GTP Steamships and renamed *Prince John*. Purchased from CN in 1940.

Dimensions: Length: 185.3', breadth 29.6', depth 11.9'. Gross tons 905.

Engines: Triple expansion, 136 NHP, 850 IHP. Speed 11 knots.

Services: Queen Charlotte Islands.

Capacities: Passenger licence 85, cabin berths 38. Cargo 400 tons.

General: Retired 1949 and scrapped in San Francisco in 1951.

Cassiar III

In Union service: 1951–1959

Type: Steel cargo vessel. Built 1946 by Burrard Dry Dock Co., North Vancouver, BC, as *Ottawa Page*. Sold to Job Bros., St. John's, Newfoundland, and renamed *Blue Peter II*. Bought by Union in 1951.

Dimensions: Length: 214.1', breadth 36.7', depth 19.8'. Gross tons 1377.

Engines: Originally triple expansion, IHP 900. Converted in 1955 to diesel (National Supply Co., Springfield, Ohio). BHP 1440. Speed 13 knots.

Capacities: Passenger licence 4. Cargo 1500 tons.

General: Renamed *Skeena Prince* by Northland in 1959.

Catala

In Union service: 1925–1959

Type: Steel twin-screw passenger–freighter. Built 1925 by Coaster Construction Co., Montrose, Scotland.

Dimensions: Length 218.0', breadth 37.1', depth 18.4'. Gross tons 1476.

Engines: Triple expansion, 200 NHP; Yarrow water-tube boilers. Speed 14 knots.

Services: Weekly on route to Prince Rupert and Stewart.

Capacities: Passenger licence 267, cabin berths 120, deck 48. Cargo 300 tons.

General: After being taken over by Northland in 1959 the *Catala* was bought by Nelson Bros. Fisheries. Later used as hotel ship during Seattle's Century 21 exposition, then moored at Gray's Harbour and wrecked by storm in 1965.

Chasina

In Union service: 1917–1923

Type: Iron passenger–freight vessel. Built 1881 by J. Elder & Co., Glasgow, as a steam yacht *Santa Cecilia*. Renamed *Selma* and bought by All-Red Line, in 1910. Renamed *Chasina* when Union took over in 1917.

Dimensions: Length 141.8', breadth 22.1', depth 11.6'. Gross tons 258.

Engines: Compound 80 RHP. Speed 13.5 knots maximum, 11.5 average.

Services: Vancouver–Powell River run.

Capacities: Summer passenger licence 200, winter 153.

Cargo 40 tons.

General: Sold in 1923 and reportedly used as a rum-runner. Resold in 1931, and, after departing from Hong Kong on September 6 of the same year, was never heard from again.

Cheslakee

In Union service: 1910–1913

Type: Steel passenger–freight vessel. Built in 1910 by Dublin Dockyard Co. and completed at Belfast.

Dimensions: Length 126.0', breadth 28.1', depth 10.0'. Gross tons 526.

Engines: MacColl & Co., triple expansion 58 RHP. Speed 12 knots maximum.

Services: Logging camps.

Capacities: Passenger licence 148, cabin berths 56. Cargo 120 tons.

General: Sank at Van Anda, Texada Island, on January 7, 1913. Lengthened by 20 ft. and renamed *Cheakamus*.

Cheakamus

In Union service: 1913–1942

Type: Steel-passenger freight vessel (see *Cheslakee*).

Dimensions: Length 145.3', breadth 28.1', depth 10.7'. Gross tons 688.

Engines: MacColl & Co., triple expansion, 58 RHP. Speed 12 knots maximum, 10.5 average.

Services: Logging camps.

Capacities: Passenger licence 148, berths 56. Cargo 120 tons.

General: Converted in 1942 into towboat. Sold the same year to US Department of Transport as a salvage tug.

Cheam

In Union service: 1920–1923

Type: Wooden twin-screw passenger–freighter. Built in 1901 as the *City of Nanaimo* by McAlpine & Allen at False Creek, Vancouver, BC. Purchased by Terminal Steam Navigation and renamed *Bowena*. Taken over by Union with the Bowen resort in 1920 and renamed *Cheam*.

Dimensions: Length 159.0', breadth 32.0', depth 9.4'. Gross tons 821.

Engines: Compound NHP 51. Speed 10.5 knots.

Services: Bowen Island–Britannia–Squamish routes.

Capacities: Summer passenger licence 500, winter 200. Cargo 200 tons.

General: Retired 1923 and scrapped in 1926.

Chehalis

In Union service: 1897–1906

Type: Wooden tug. Built 1897 by C. McAlpine, False Creek, Vancouver, BC.

Dimensions: Length 59.7', breadth 13.3', depth 6.5'. Gross tons 54.

Engines: Bow McLachlan (from *Skidegate*).

Services: Towing contracts.

General: Sank on July 12, 1906, in a collision in First Narrows; eight crew and passengers drowned.

Chelan

In Union service: 1952–1954

Type: Steel tug and cargo motor vessel. Built 1944 by Northwestern Shipbuilding Co., Bellingham, Wash., for the US Navy, and later named *Veta C*. Renamed *Chelan* after Union purchase.

Dimensions: Length 148.0', breadth 33.3', depth 15.6'. Gross tons 541.

Engines: Diesel. Speed 12 knots.

Services: Towed bulk concentrates.

Capacities: Cargo 450 tons.

General: Lost with crew of 14 off Cape Decision, Alaska, while towing *Bulk Carrier No. 2* from Skagway on April 15, 1954.

Chelohsin
In Union service: 1911–1949
Type: Steel twin screw passenger freight vessel. Built 1911 at Dublin Dockyard Co., Ireland, and completed at Belfast.
Dimensions: Length 175.5', breadth 35.1', depth 14.0'. Gross tons 1134.
Engines: Triple expansion, IHP 1420, MacColl & Co., Belfast. Two multi-tubular boilers amidships. Speed 14 knots maximum, 12.5 average.
Services: On Prince Rupert run, then on main logging camp routes to Port Hardy.
Capacities: Passenger licence 191, cabin berths 66, deck settees 95. Cargo 150 tons.
General: One of the Union's most popular ships. Ran aground outside Vancouver harbour November 4, 1949. Dismantled in 1951.

Chenega
In Union service: 1954–1959
Type: Steel cargo motor vessel. Built 1916 by Anderson Steamboat Co., Seattle, as lighthouse tender *Rose*. Bought by Union in 1954 as the *Northern Express* from General Sea Transportation Ltd., then dieselized and renamed *Chenega*.
Dimensions: Length 129.3', breadth 24.6', depth 11.0'. Gross tons 381.
Engines: Repowered in 1956 with twin GM diesels. Speed 12 knots.
Services: Northern BC cargo routes.
Capacities: Cargo 350 tons, including refrigeration space.

Chilco & Lady Pam
In Union service: 1917–1935 as the *Chilco*. Renamed *Lady Pam* and continued in service 1935–1946.
Type: Steel passenger–freight vessel. Built 1883 by J. Elder & Co., Glasgow, as steam yacht *Santa Maria*. Obtained by Union with purchase of All-Red Line in 1917.
Dimensions: Length 151.0', breadth 22.0', depth 12.6'. Gross tons 305.
Engines: Direct-acting, compound 80 RHP. Speed 13 knots, 11.5 average.
Services: Vancouver–Powell River run as *Chilco*; the *Lady Pam* worked in Howe Sound.
Capacities: Summer passenger licence as the *Chilco* 200, winter 144; as the *Lady Pam*, 130 all year. Cargo 40 tons.
General: Retired in 1946, then used as a breakwater at Oyster Bay, south of Campbell River.

Chilcotin
In Union service: 1947–1958
Type: Steel passenger–freight vessel. Built 1944 by Henry Robb Ltd., Leith, Scotland, as Castle-class corvette HMS *Hespeler*.
Dimensions: Length 235.7', breadth 36.6', depth 22.2'. Gross tons 1837.
Engines: Triple expansion, IHP 2800. Speed 15 knots.
Services: Alaska summer cruises.
Capacities: Passenger licence 200, first class berths 106. Cargo 250 tons.
General: Sold to Sun Line, Monrovia, in February, 1958 and renamed *Capri*. Later refitted for cruises from the St. Lawrence as *Stella Maris*. Destroyed by fire at Sardinia.

Chilkoot I
In Union service: 1920–1934
Type: Steel freighter. Built by Wallace Shipbuilding Co., North Vancouver, in 1920.
Dimensions: Length 172.6', breadth 30.2', depth 12.9'. Gross tons 756.
Engines: Inverted vertical triple, IHP 725, from Builders Iron Foundry, Providence, USA. Speed 12 knots maximum.
Capacities: Cargo 800 tons (2000 cases of salmon or 400M ft. of lumber). Passenger licence 12, cabin berths 2.
General: Sold to Border Line in 1934; later to BC Steamships (Northland) and dieselized as *Alaska Prince*.

Chilkoot II
In Union service: 1946–1957
Type: Steel freighter, China-coaster type. Taken over by Union while under construction at Victoria Machinery Depot, Victoria, BC, and completed 1946.
Dimensions: Length 214.1', breadth 36.7', depth 19.9'. Gross tons 1336.
Engines: Single, triple expansion IHP 900. Speed 11 knots.
Services: Port Alice cargo and pulp route.
Capacities: Passenger licence 4. Cargo 1500 tons.
General: The last of the Union's freighters. Sold in 1957 to Navieros Unidos Del Pacifico S.A., Mazatlan, Mexico.

Chilliwack I
In Union service: 1919–1926
Type: Steel freighter. Built 1903 by Scott & Co., Bowling, Scotland, as the *Onyx* and renamed *British Columbia* by Coastwise Tugboat & Barge Co. Bought by Union in January 1919 and renamed *Chilliwack*.
Dimensions: Length 170.7', breadth 27.0', depth 12.9'. Gross tons 557.
Engines: Triple expansion, 81 NHP. Scotch marine boilers built by Ross & Duncan. Speed 9 knots.
Services: Cannery trade and bulk ore.
Capacities: Cargo 750 tons (15,000 cases of salmon or 325M ft. of lumber). Passenger licence 10, berths 4.
General: Retired in 1926. Sold to Goose Packing Co. as a floating cannery.

Chilliwack II
In Union service: 1927–1954
Type: Steel screw freighter. Built 1917 as the *Ardgarvel* by Ferguson Bros., Port Glasgow. Bought by Union in 1927 and renamed *Chilliwack II*.
Dimensions: Length 200.3', breadth 30.2', depth 12.8'. Gross tons 834.
Engines: Triple expansion, NHP 90. Speed 10 knots.
Capacities: Passenger licence 10, berths 4. Cargo 1100 tons.
General: Sold in 1954 to the Micronesia Metal & Equipment Co., and renamed *Iron Shield*.

Island King & Chilliwack III
In Union service: 1944–1954 as *Island King*. Renamed *Chilliwack III*, continued in service 1954–1959.
Type: Steel cargo motor vessel. Built in 1920 by Trosvik Mer. Verk at Brevik, Norway, as the *Granit* and later named *Columbia*.
Dimensions: Length 165.1', breadth 28.2', depth 12.4'. Gross tons 591.
Engines: Diesel BHP 400. Speed 10 knots.
Services: Port Alice and general routes.
Capacities: Passenger licence 4, increased to 12 in 1958. Cargo 800 tons.
General: Renamed *Tahsis Prince* by Northland in 1959.

Comox I

In Union service: 1891–1919
Type: Steel screw passenger–freighter. Hull prefabricated in sections by J. McArthur & Co., Glasgow. Launched from Union shipyard in Vancouver's Coal Harbour in 1891.
Dimensions: Length 101.0', breadth 18.1', depth 5.2'. Gross tons 101.
Engines: Bow McLachlan & Co., Paisley, Scotland. Compound 28 RHP. Speed 12 knots.
Services: Logging camps.
Capacities: Passenger licence 200; 40 berths after rebuild in 1897. Cargo 100 tons.
General: First steel ship launched in BC (October 24, 1891). Pioneer Union vessel on logging camp runs.

Comox II

In Union service: 1924–1943
Type: Wooden passenger–freight motor vessel. Built 1924 by Wallace Shipbuilding Co., North Vancouver.
Dimensions: Length 54.0', breadth 15.5', depth 7.2'. Gross tons 54.
Engines: Diesel Atlas Imperial, Oakland, Calif., 3 cylinders, BHP 55. Speed 7 knots.
Services: Used intermittently on Pender Harbour–Jervis Inlet runs.
Capacities: Passenger licence 25. Cargo 15 tons (approx.).

Coquitlam I

In Union service: 1892–1923
Type: Steel screw freighter–passenger vessel. Hull prefabricated in sections by J. McArthur & Co., Glasgow. Launched from Union shipyard in Coal Harbour in 1892.
Dimensions: Length 120.0', breadth 22.0', depth 9.6'. Gross tons 256.
Engines: Bow McLachlan & Co., Paisley, Scotland. Compound 28 RHP. Speed 10 knots maximum, 9 average.
Capacities: Passenger licence 24 (deck); rebuilt for Alaskan service in 1897 to provide 93 berths with licence 157. Cargo 300 tons.
General: Became centre of an international dispute when seized by US Customs on June 22, 1892. Sold to Bervin SS Co. in 1923. Returned to Union fleet (with Frank Waterhouse & Co. ships) in 1939. Sold to Canadian Fishing Co. in 1950. Beached at Malcolm Island as breakwater in 1959.

Coquitlam II

In Union service: 1946–1958
Type: Steel passenger–freight vessel. Built in 1943 by Smith's Dock Co., Middlesbrough, England as Castle-class corvette HMS *St. Thomas*. Converted in 1946 by Burrard Dry Dock Co., North Vancouver, BC.
Dimensions: Length 235.7', breadth 36.6', depth 22.2'. Gross tons 1835.
Engines: Triple expansion, IHP 2,800. Speed 15 knots maximum.
Services: Northern BC and Alaskan cruise service.
Capacities: Passenger licence 200, berths 114, deck 16. Cargo 250 tons.
General: Sold in 1958 to Alaska Cruise Lines and renamed *Glacier Queen*.

Coutli

In Union service: 1904–1909
Type: Wooden tug. Built 1904 by George E. Cates, False Creek, Vancouver, BC.
Dimensions: Length 71.4', breadth 18.8'. Gross tons 99.
Engines: Compound. Bow McLachlan, Paisley, Scotland, 1903.
Services: Towing contracts.
General: The last Union tug. Sold in 1910 to the Red Fir Lumber Co., Nanaimo, BC.

Cowichan

In Union service: 1908–1925
Type: Steel passenger–freight vessel. Built 1908 by Ailsa Shipbuilding Co., Troon, Scotland. Launched as *Cariboo*, but name changed when registry duplication discovered after arrival on Pacific coast.
Dimensions: Length 156.1', breadth 32.0', depth 13.5'. Gross tons 961.
Engines: Twin triple expansion, 116 NHP, built by MacColl & Co. Two multi-tubular boilers, built by D. Rowan & Co. Speed 11 knots.
Services: Main logging camp routes.
Capacities: Passenger licence 165, cabin berths 53. Cargo 125 tons.
General: Sank in fog collision with *Lady Cynthia* on December 27, 1925.

Cutch

In Union service: 1890–1900
Type: Iron screw passenger–freight vessel. Built as a steam yacht in 1884 by J. Bremner & Co., Hull, England, for Indian prince. Purchased by Union in 1890.
Dimensions: Length: 180.0', breadth 23.0', depth 11.7'. Gross tons 324.
Engines: Compound 25" and 48" x 30". Speed 13 knots.
Services: Vancouver–Nanaimo and Vancouver–Skagway (1898–1900).
Capacities: Passenger licence 150. Cargo 150 tons.
General: Wrecked south of Juneau, Alaska August 24, 1900. Rebuilt 1901 as *Jessie Banning*. Converted to warship *Bogota* in 1902 for Columbia in Peru conflict. Scrapped and sunk in South America.

Eastholm

In Union service: 1939–1957
Type: Wooden freighter. Built 1913 by A. Moscrop, Vancouver, BC and taken over with Waterhouse Co. fleet in 1939.
Dimensions: Length 93.0', breadth 24.3', depth 6.8'. Gross tons 174.
Engines: Single, 16 NHP. Speed 8 knots.
Services: Local cargo service and contracts.
Capacities: Cargo 250 tons.

Gray

In Union service: 1939–1944
Type: Steel freighter. Built 1909 by R. Williamson & Son, Workington, England, as the Petriana. Operated on BC coast in 1910 by Northern Steamships, and obtained by Union in 1939 purchase of Waterhouse Co.
Dimensions: Length 182.7', breadth 27.9', depth 12.3'. Gross tons 707.
Engines: Single, 90 RHP. Speed 9 knots.
Capacities: Cargo 650 tons.
General: Sold in 1946.

Lady Cecilia

In Union service: 1925–1951
Type: Steel twin-screw passenger freighter. Built in 1919 as minesweeper HMS Swindon and converted in 1925 by Coaster Construction Co., Montrose, Scotland, for the Union.
Dimensions: Length 235.0', breadth 28.6', depth 16.3'. Gross tons 944.
Engines: Triple expansion, NHP 250, IHP 1600; Yarrow boilers. Speed 15.5 maximum, 13.5 average.

Services: Gulf coast and Howe Sound routes.
Capacities: Summer passenger licence 800, winter 500.
Cargo 75 tons.
General: Retired in 1951.

Lady Alexandra
In Union service: 1924–1954
Type: Steel twin-screw passenger and freight vessel. Built 1924 by Coaster Construction Co., Montrose, Scotland.
Dimensions: Length 225.4', breadth 40.1', depth 9.7'. Gross tons 1396.
Engines: Reciprocating steam triple expansion, two engines NHP 270, IHP 2,000; Yarrow water-tube boilers. Speed 14 knots.
Services: To Bowen Island resort; twice-weekly evening dance cruises and a variety of excursions.
Capacities: Passenger licence 1400 (Howe Sound) 900 (Victoria). Cargo 300 tons.
General: Vancouver's premier excursion vessel. After being laid up in 1954 the *Lady Alex* was sold to become a floating restaurant in Coal Harbour. Scuttled in March 1980 at Redondo Beach, Calif, after listing in a severe storm.

Lady Cynthia
In Union service: 1925–1957
Type: Steel twin-screw passenger–freighter. Built 1919 as the minesweeper HMS *Barnstable* at Ardrossan, Scotland. Converted in 1925 by the Coaster Construction Co., Montrose, Scotland, as the *Lady Cynthia*.
Dimensions: Length 235.0', breadth 28.6, depth 16.3'. Gross tons 950.
Engines: Triple expansion, NHP 250, IHP 1,600; Yarrow boilers. Speed 15.5 knots maximum, 13.5 average.
Services: Mainly on Bowen Island–Squamish route.
Capacities: Summer passenger licence 800, winter 500. Cargo 75 tons.
General: Sold in 1951 to Coast Ferries and scrapped in Seattle in 1957.

Lady Evelyn
In Union service: 1923–1936
Type: Steel twin-screw passenger–freighter. Built 1901 as the *Deerhound* by J. Jones & Sons at Birkenhead for the West Cornwall SS Co. Later engaged in the St. Lawrence mail run. Bought by Union from Howe Sound Navigation in 1923.
Dimensions: Length 189.0', breadth 26.1', depth 9.5'. Gross tons 588.
Engines: Triple expansion, NHP 150, IHP 1,500, two engines. Speed 14 knots maximum, 13 average.
Services: West Howe Sound and Gulf coast.
Capacities: Summer passenger licence 480, winter 200. Cargo 100 tons.
General: Laid up at Bidwell Bay and scrapped in 1936.

Lady Rose
In Union service: 1937–1951
Type: Steel passenger and cargo motor vessel. Built 1937 by A. & J. Inglis Ltd., Glasgow; launched as the *Lady Sylvia* but renamed *Lady Rose* due to duplication.
Dimensions: Length 104.8', breadth 21.2', depth 14.3'. Gross tons 199.
Engines: Diesel. One 220 BHP propelling unit and one 28 BHP auxiliary, National Gas & Oil Co., England. Speed 11.5 knots.
Capacities: Summer passenger licence 130, winter 70. Cargo 25 tons.
General: Sold to Harbour Navigation Co. in 1951. The *Lady Rose* is still in service on the west coast of Vancouver Island.

Leonora
In Union service: 1889–1904
Type: Wooden tug. Built 1876 at Moodyville and completed in Victoria.
Dimensions: Length 57.0', breadth 9.0', depth 5.3'. Gross tons 33.
Engines: 15 NHP, supplied by Albion Iron Works, Victoria, BC. Speed approximately 7 knots.
Services: Moodyville ferry and Vancouver harbour towing.
Capacities: Passengers approx. 25. Cargo 5 tons.
General: Wrecked off Cracroft Island in 1919.

Melmore
In Union service: 1914–1916
Type: Steel twin-screw passenger–freight vessel. Built in 1892 and operated between Glasgow and Northern Ireland ports. Brought to Vancouver in 1913. Purchased by Union in 1914 and converted for excursion trade.
Dimensions: Length 156.0', breadth 26.0', depth 11.3'. Gross tons 424.
Engines: Compound, 96 RHP. Speed 12 knots.
Services: Summer excursions, and evening trips to Howe Sound.
Capacities: Passenger licence 475. Cargo 50 tons.
General. Operated as Union boat in summer of 1914 only. Sold to Peru in 1916 and renamed *Santa Elena*.

Northholm
In Union service: 1939–1943
Type: Steel freighter. Built 1924 by J. Towers Shipbuilding, Bristol, as the *Robert H. Merrick*. Taken over with Waterhouse Co. by Union in 1939.
Dimensions: Length 150.2', breadth 25.2', depth 11.9'. Gross tons 447.
Engines: Single, 81 RHP. Speed 10 knots.
Capacities: 550 tons.
General: Foundered in gale off Cape Scott on January 16, 1943, with loss of 15 of 17 crew.

Redonda
In Union service: 1955–1959
Type: Steel diesel cargo tanker, landing ship class. Built 1944 at Portland, Ore. as USS *YTC No. 501-52*.
Dimensions: Length 125.0', breadth 23.6', depth 6.6'. Gross tons 185.
Engines: Diesel. Speed 7 knots.
Services: Logging camps.
Capacities: Cargo 225 tons.

Senator
In Union service: 1889–1904
Type: Wooden tug. Completed in Moodyville, BC in 1881.
Dimensions: Length 51.5', breadth 12.0'. depth 4.5'. Gross tons 31.
Engines: Double engines 7 1/4" X 8", from Albion Iron Works, Victoria, BC. Speed 8 knots.
Services: Moodyville ferry.
Capacities: Passenger licence 30.
General: Sunk in Manson's Deep off Bowen Island in 1925.

Skidegate
In Union service: 1889–1897
Type: Wooden tug. Built 1879 at Victoria, BC as cannery tender. Rebuilt 1891 as passenger–freight vessel.
Dimensions: Length 76.0', breadth 12.5', depth 6.0'. Gross tons 37.
Engines: New Bow McLachlan engines (11" and 22" x 14"). Speed 11 knots.

Capacities: Passenger licence 20. Cargo approximately 20 tons.
General. Removed from service in 1897 and broken up. Engines installed in *Chehalis.*

Southholm
In Union service: 1939–1950
Type: Steel freighter. Built 1919 by Canadian Car & Foundry, Fort William, Ont. as the *E.D. Kingsley.* Taken over with the Waterhouse Co. by Union in 1939.
Dimensions: Length 200.0', breadth 32.0', depth 14.5'. Gross tons 1029.
Engines: Single, 825 IHP. Speed 10 knots.
Capacities: Cargo 1100 tons.
General: Converted in 1950 into barge *Bulk Carrier No. 1.*

Tournament
In Union service: 1956–1959
Type: Steel passenger and freight motor ship. Built at Annapolis Boatyard, City Island, New York, in 1942, and named *Jervis Express* before purchase by Tidewater Co.
Dimensions: Length 108.0', breadth 18.4', depth 7.0'. Gross tons 149.
Engines: Twin diesels. Speed 15 knots maximum, 13 average.
Capacities: Passenger licence 101. Cargo 40 tons.

Troubadour III
In Union service: 1956–1959
Type: Steel diesel passenger vessel and packet freighter. Built in 1944 by Star Shipyard, New Westminster, BC. Converted and named *Gulf-Wing* by Gulf Lines Ltd. 1946. Bought by Tidewater Co. 1952 and renamed *Troubadour.*
Dimensions: Length 107.6', breadth 18.0', depth 6.0'. Gross tons 103.
Engines: Two 320 HP V-diesels. Speed 15 knots.
Capacities: Passenger licence 95. Cargo 25 tons.

Triggerfish
In Union service: 1956
Type: Steel cargo motor ship. Built by G. Hittebrant, Kingston, NY.
Dimensions: Length 108.0', breadth 18.4', depth 8.0'. Gross tons 149.
Engines: Diesel. Speed 10 knots.
Services: Logging route.
Capacities: Cargo 100 tons.
General: Sank off Whytecliff on October 6, 1956 with loss of 3 crew.

Vadso
In Union service: 1911–1914
Type: Steel freighter and passenger vessel. Built in 1881 at Motala, Sweden, as the *Bordeaux.* Purchased in 1907 by Boscowitz Co. and renamed *Vadso.* Taken over by Union in 1911.
Dimensions: Length 191.2', breadth 28.7', depth 21.7'. Gross tons 908.
Engines: Compound. Speed 11 knots.
Services: Northern cannery trade.
Capacities: Passenger licence 50. Cargo 400 tons.
General: Wrecked and burned near mouth of Nass River, February 3, 1914.

Venture
In Union service: 1911–1946
Type: Steel twin-screw passenger–freight vessel. Built in 1910 by Napier & Miller, Old Kilpatrick, Scotland, for Boscowitz Co. Taken over by Union in 1911.
Dimensions: Length 180.4', breadth 32.0', depth 17.0'. Gross tons 1011.
Engines: Direct-acting, triple expansion, IHP 1150, built by Miller & Macfie. Speed 13 knots.
Services: Northern cannery route.
Capacities: Passenger licence 186, cabin berths 60, deck settees, 85. Cargo 550 tons.
General: An excellent sea boat. Sold to Chinese firm in 1946 and renamed *Hsin Kong So.* Destroyed by fire at Hong Kong in 1947.

Washington
In Union service: 1918
Type: Steel passenger–freight vessel. Built 1914 at Dockton, WA.
Dimensions: Length 125.5', breadth 25.8', depth 7.3'. Gross tons 306.
Engines: Triple expansion, NHP 51, built by Hutton, Seattle. Speed 12 knots.
Services: Used briefly on Sechelt excursions.
Capacities: Passenger licence 350. Cargo approximately 50 tons.
General: Hull resold after engines removed.

Bulk Carriers (Barges)
Bulk Carrier Union No. 1 (Ex-*Southholm*)
Bulk Carrier Union No. 2 (Ex-*Princess Mary*)
Bulk Carrier Union No. 3 (Ex-USS *A.R.R. 742* [landing ship])
Bulk Carrier Barge Taku (*Princess Maquinna*)

Index